This book comes at the perfect time in a context where youth represent most of Africa's population. It provides clear and practical answers to their questions in their quest for change. Sure, we all want change, but as Christians we must not forget that true Christian leadership cannot work without God at the centre of leaders' lives. Being a true Christian leader requires you to first be influenced by God before influencing others. A book to be read and taught to the new generation.

— Dr Daniel Kouakou,
Faculty Member of The John Maxwell Team (Côte d'Ivoire)

This little book is succinct and helpful encouragement for problem-solving and causing change for the better, in your family, workplace, or community. A common leadership challenge is resistance to change, especially when those with position and power put a lid on change. Positional authority alone could be stagnant. Titles and positions by themselves may not effectively deliver permanent transformation.

Morrison and Gaya demonstrate how one could lead from behind. Leading or influencing change without any authority to enforce this but causing those with the 'power and authority' to take off the lid and gladly embrace the change—leadership at its best.

This kind of leadership is not only intergenerational but encourages every person to pour into others what God has graciously endowed each one of us with—influence. A helpful tool to influence change for the better in your sphere of influence and the society as a whole.

— Rev Dr Aiah Foday-Khabenje,
General Secretary of the Association of Evangelicals in Africa,
author of *Competencies in Leading in Diversity* (Sierra Leone)

Gaya is a testimony to the fact that having influence in life has little or nothing to do with positional authority. He has much influence among his peers and impresses those who are older than him. In Africa that is BIG! Having invested in his life, I can say that some of the nuggets of truth in this book are practical testimonies he lives out in his daily leadership journey. I highly commend this book to everyone who desires to make a difference in the world. It is biblical, theologically balanced, compelling, and filled with practical stories.

— Rev Gideon Para-Mallam,
Continental Mission Leader and Social Justice Peace Advocate, former Regional Secretary of the International Fellowship of Evangelical Students in English- and Portuguese-Speaking Africa (Nigeria)

Morrison and Gaya explain how ordinary people can influence those in leadership. One does not need to hold an official position or title to influence people to accomplish God's purposes for one's life and community. Influence over others results from application of values and principles that motivate change. They support their arguments with examples from their own lives and ministry experience and biblical models of young leaders and ordinary people who influenced their mentors and leaders.

I highly recommend this book to mature leaders who desire to multiply themselves, as well as young leaders and any Christian hoping to make a difference in their church and community in Africa and beyond.

— Prof Faustin Ntamushobora,
President & CEO of Transformational Leadership in Africa (Rwanda)

I am a great admirer of Phil Morrison and his books. Like his other books, *Influence* is as compelling as it is practical. It blends biblical and real-life examples seamlessly. When I started reading it, I couldn't stop. It is so boldly refreshing and touches both the mind and the heart in new ways. It is desperately needed at this time when many Christian leaders are failing to lead through influence, opting for meaningless titles and positions. I enthusiastically endorse the book as a core resource for leaders and aspiring leaders in both formal and informal leadership positions.

— Dr Joy Mbaabu, Lawyer, Mediator,
Conflict Resolver, and Peacemaker (Kenya)

Morrison and Gaya have given us something special – a tutor on how to lead without position. It is easy to read, with interesting, relatable stories from real life. A key theme that runs through the whole book is that anyone can lead by influencing, as long as one has the right attitude, character, and knowledge. Young people in Africa, take advantage of this special tool. It is something we wish we had when we were young. To the older generation, I have learned some exciting things from this book. Let us use them while we still can. It is not yet too late!

— Pastor Chris Mwalwa,
Word of Life Fellowship and Africa Inland Church,
Ngong Road, Nairobi (Kenya)

# INFLUENCE

## LEADING WITHOUT POSITION

PHILIP E. MORRISON AND HANKURI TAWUS GAYA

INSIGHT BOOKS
AFRICAN ISSUES AFRICA'S AUTHORS

OASIS INTERNATIONAL PUBLISHING

This book is dedicated to all those who desire to make
a difference in the life of their church, home,
workplace, campus, culture, society, and country,
whether they have an official leadership position or not.

**Influence: Leading Without Position**

With contributions from Hankuri Tawus Gaya.



ISBN 13: 978-1-59452-766-1
ISBN: 1-59452-766-0

Published by Oasis International Ltd.

**Oasis International is a ministry devoted to growing discipleship through publishing African voices.**

- We *engage* Africa's most influential, most relevant, and best communicators for the sake of the gospel
- We *cultivate* local and global partnerships in order to publish and distribute high-quality books and Bibles
- We *create* contextual content that meets the specific needs of Africa, has the power to transform individuals and societies, and gives the church in Africa a global voice

Oasis is: *Satisfying Africa's Thirst for God's Word*. For more information, go to oasisinternational.com.





20 21 22 23 24 25 BPI 10 9 8 7 6 5 4 3 2 1

# CONTENTS

# ACKNOWLEDGEMENTS

**Philip E. Morrison:**

Thanks to my daughter, Emily, for her good suggestions, careful reading, and initial editing of the manuscript. A lot of red ink was used on that first draft! I am grateful. And thanks also to Beatrice Sijenyi who volunteered to do additional proofreading.

A special thanks to Sandy Morad, my Unit Leader, who has been a great supporter of both my teaching and writing ministry and who encouraged me in the writing of this book by granting permission to periodically take writing retreats to concentrate on the completion of this and other writing projects.

Thanks to Hannah Rasmussen, our Oasis editor, for her careful attention to this revised edition and shepherding the manuscript through the whole publishing process.

Thanks to my wife, Jan, who is my life partner and friend. Your love, support, and patience with me in my many weaknesses and shortcomings is amazing.

Finally, thanks to Jesus Christ, my Lord and Saviour, who never held an official leadership position while here on earth, and yet whose brief life has had the biggest influence on world history and humankind. I look forward to the day when he will return and set up his kingdom on earth. "And he will reign forever and ever." Hallelujah!

**Hankuri Tawus Gaya:**

I appreciate the Lord for the opportunity given to me to learn and write. Thanks to the Oasis team, especially Hannah Rasmussen the acquisitions editor, for the great work they did on editing the book and making it available. To Uncle Phil, I appreciate you for initiating this project and inviting me to join you in your writing.

Your passion for Africa and leadership in the church is worth emulating.

Thanks to the Nigeria Fellowship of Evangelical Students (NIFES) leadership and senior staff team for providing leadership as we keep on investing in shaping students on campus. Special thanks to Muyiwa Joseph and Anita Ambi, who created time to listen to some of my thoughts before sharing them on the book, and the entire staff team I work with in NIFES Bauchi and Keffi Area.

Thanks to my parents Lt. Pastor Tawus G. Gaya and Bilhatu T. Gaya for the training and exposure they gave to me even when it did not make sense and for all their sacrifices over the years. To all my siblings I say thank you.

Thanks also to all my leaders and mentors in student ministry and leaders in church for creating an opportunity for me to learn.

Faith, my wife and dear friend, has been a loving support to my life, ministry, and writing passion – thank you. To our children, Gift-Vinawar, Peace-Shisa, and Joy-Khalla, your love and support has brought me this far. I appreciate you.

INTRODUCTION

# LEADING IS INFLUENCE

While positional power is helpful to the leader, it is not required. That is because a greater power can be found in the influence of one's life, character, and relationships.[1]

—— GARY BREDFELDT ——

## OUR STORIES

**Hankuri:** I grew up in the church as a pastor's kid in north-eastern Nigeria. As a teenager I had a passion for God's Word and I also had ideas for solving problems around me. When I joined the Nigeria Fellowship of Evangelical Students (NIFES) as an undergraduate, I learned further how to study the Scriptures inductively, apply them to life, and live out the principles of biblical leadership. I was excitedly looking forward to applying these lessons to make a difference in my country.

Then I went home for the holidays. In the church my father pastored, we had nothing like Bible studies. Preachers often did not interpret the Scriptures properly and sometimes the context of a passage was completely ignored. At the same time, the issues people were facing weren't addressed. Here I was, seated in the congregation with training on how to study God's Word and apply the Scriptures to practical living, and yet because of my age I was neither allowed to lead services nor preach in my home church.

Approaching my father was not an option. I felt like to him I was still a small boy growing up. So I decided to share my thoughts and ideas with some elders in the church and in the community. I suggested that we begin Bible study classes, create a forum to teach people on topics affecting them, and allow the youth to gain life skills by being more involved in the church and the community. They responded with the attitude: "Wait for your time and watch against pride. This is our time to lead."

I was crushed. I wanted so badly to contribute to the growth of the body of Christ, but I felt the leaders were not interested in developing the youth or the church's future. Nothing is more frustrating than believing you have a solution to a problem but not being allowed to implement it because of culture and church tradition.

> Nothing is more frustrating than believing you have a solution to a problem but not being allowed to implement it.

Many of us feel like we are in this position at times. We have ideas, but we can't do anything about them. Perhaps, like in my case, people say we are too young or inexperienced. In many of our African cultures and contexts, young people have little say. They must listen to and obey parents and elders of the church and the community. Yet over half of Africa's population is under the age of 20, and young people are facing different challenges than the older generation. The older generation sits in the decision-making seats, and often they do not have meaningful dialogue with or listen to those they are leading. Undoubtedly, we have all experienced a leader who dismissed the concerns of the young and felt threatened by younger influencers.

But this sense of powerlessness doesn't affect just the young. People in entry-level positions, evangelists in the church, or other junior staff may feel they are burdened with many responsibilities without having the support they need or contributing to important decisions. Women are also often overlooked for leadership positions, although half the population of the continent is female. This is especially common in church settings. In many organizations and churches, one's tribal identity or family connections determine who has influence and position rather than one's qualifications, leaving out many potential leaders. Even if you have a formal leadership in one context, you may find yourself frustrated and wanting to make a change in another setting.

So in some way most, if not all of us, will find ourselves participating in an organization or a group where we do not have an official position of leadership. How can we bring positive change when it seems we have no power or respect?

**Phil:** In my 26 years in Kenya, I frequently met people who wondered how they could make a difference. I taught future pastors in Bible college who were eager to bring about change in their denominations and local churches. Through The Multi-Church Pastor Institute (the seminar ministry I founded), I taught untrained and undertrained pastors basic church leadership skills to bring about change and revitalization of their ministries in eight African countries. What I often found was that people were disqualified or shut out of church leadership even when they had the skills and abilities required, simply because they didn't have the right connections, age, gender, or ethnicity.

In my doctoral studies in Transformational Leadership, we spent time working through the issue of how leaders can bring about organizational change. However, in my own experience, I found that often those in leadership positions were not always interested in bringing about change in their churches and ministries. Furthermore, they were often not open to the ideas of those who desired things to be different and relevant to the rapidly changing culture and society of Africa. To my mind, this attitude could only lead to an increasing irrelevancy and ineffectiveness of the church in ministering to contemporary culture and of reaching the current generation with the gospel. As a result, the church would be increasingly ignored and viewed as impotent in addressing the challenges of modern life.

This caused me to ask, if many present leaders were not willing to work for change, who would and how could it be done? I realized change had to come through those who were motivated to improve their communities and were willing to be used to influence others in the process. And these were often those who were marginalized by the present leaders and who thought that because they did not have a position, they could not lead.

**Hankuri:** Since my student days I have learned how I can change my approach so as not to come across as proud to the church elders. But I have also learned that I don't just have to wait for my time. Part of my frustration as a young person came from my mistaken belief that I needed a position to influence change. Through reading the Scriptures, books, and stories of leaders, my perspective on influence has changed. I now know principles that you can apply to begin to have influence right where you are, regardless of your position or standing. I have even learned how to influence my leaders and work with them, benefitting from their experience, wisdom, and resources to come up with real solutions to the issues Africa is facing.

My experiences have made me passionate about mentoring young people to be leaders right where they are. For the last 12 years, I have worked with students in tertiary institutions in the ministry of Nigeria Fellowship of Evangelical Students (NIFES). This organization is part of the larger International Fellowship of Evangelical Students (IFES), which includes groups such as InterVarsity in the USA. I mentor and empower students to lead their campus fellowships. I also try to shape their mindsets for leadership, knowing that when they finish their education they might find harsh leaders in their workplaces and churches. By God's grace, I have been able to watch these students make a difference in society.

Both of us know many people with brilliant ideas about how to transform their communities. We are convinced that our continent needs your ideas and you to take initiative to solve its problems. Our goal in this book is to encourage anyone with a desire for things to be better. This book offers tools to show you how you can be an influence to bring about change.

## A LEADER IS NOT SOMEONE WITH A POSITION OR TITLE

How will you make a difference when there are so few leadership positions and no one wants to give them up? We believe we have discovered the solution: you don't need a position to lead.

The idea might sound strange or disappointing. You might not believe that you can lead without a position. But perhaps that is because we don't understand what leadership is. Most of us think of leadership as a title.

> You don't need a position to lead.

Many of us are like the primary school pupil who said his dream was to become a governor. We yearn for titles and positions. People can pursue doctoral studies to be called "Dr", others refuse to answer when they are not addressed appropriately as "Rev", "Apostle", or "Prophet". It is good that our cultures honour leaders, respectfully calling them by their appropriate names, giving them seats of honour, special food, and compensating them.

However, some people consider the perks that come with positions – fancy transportation, financial benefits, and respect that leaders receive – and want to be leaders just for the special treatment. We must remember that we honour leaders for serving the people and treat them well for the burden they take on, so they must be held accountable to actually serve the people. I wonder how many of us, when we say we want to be leaders, know what we want to lead or what we will do when we become leaders. We just want to be somebody important. Some of us wait until we get a title before we start leading, and then we wonder why we are going nowhere.

But is leadership really about a title? Anyone can give themselves a title or get a fake degree. We have seen many politicians, bishops, and other big men in leadership positions who have not led people anywhere.

A pastor friend of mine (Phil's) tells the story of when he was the youngest and smallest member of a bunch of boys who used to hang out together in his village. One day they were standing around discussing what they should do next. It took a while, but after they had decided, my friend shouted, "Come on guys, let's go!" and he took off running down the street. He had only taken a few steps when he turned around and saw that all of the bigger boys were just standing there watching him! They weren't following him at all!

You see, he had wanted to be a leader but he wasn't. He wanted the others to follow him, but they didn't. He was part of the group, and he wanted to be the leader. But because there was no "followership" there was no leadership. Now, was the problem that my friend lacked a title or a position to make him a leader? No, the problem was that he was unable to influence the rest of the boys to follow him, so he was not their leader.

Even among people who hold official positions, many would find themselves in the same situation if they were removed from their post. You may have a title of leadership, but if your position is the only reason people follow you, then you are not really a leader.

## LEADING IS INFLUENCE

Many leaders get things done by coercion, not leadership. Most leaders try to push people, according to James O'Toole.[2] They may use harsh commands or direct force. But they may also use manipulation or subtle pressure to force people to do what they want. But anyone can do that if they have a big enough threat or a scary weapon. If leading is only about making somebody else do what you want, then even an armed robber is a leader.

But how do you get people to follow you without forcing them or using the power of a position? John Maxwell's definition is instructive: "Leadership is influence. Nothing more, nothing less." As O'Toole puts it, the best leaders lead "by the pull of inspiring values".[3]

Influence, according to the Merriam-Webster dictionary online, is "the power to cause changes without directly forcing them to happen".[4] Influence is the ability to bring about change in another's beliefs, thoughts, actions, or behaviour. Influence is demonstrated when people will listen to you, believe in the cause you are advocating, and begin to move in the direction you are encouraging them to go.

Influence is not manipulation but inspiration. Instead of convincing someone to change by tricking or pressuring them, you help them realize what is good. They change because they want to change.[5] Influence involves emphasizing the values and principles that motivate change. Using values instead of position to influence people leads to significant and lasting transformation. As Jesus said, the greatest leaders in the kingdom are to be servants of all (Mark 10:43-45).

Influence is why musicians have more followers than presidents of nations. Influence is why a poor caregiver like Mother Theresa had more global recognition than heads of multinational companies. Influence is what made Nelson Mandela of South Africa, Kwame Nkrumah of Ghana, and Chinua Achebe of Nigeria into leaders who shaped the world.

## INFLUENCED BY GOD TO INFLUENCE THE WORLD

As Christian influencers, what should we influence people toward? Should followers become just like their leader? Or should they become something unique and better?

The task of Christian leaders is not about making people follow you, or even follow your vision. People may follow you and your vision, but the goal is for them to follow God and his purposes.[6] As the apostle Paul said, "Follow my example, as I follow the example of Christ" (1 Corinthians 11:1). We define Christian leadership as: being influenced by God to become the person you are created to be, then influencing others to become what God desires them to be.

Christian leadership is being influenced by God to become the person you are created to be, then influencing others to become who God desires them to be.

In Nairobi craft markets, one commonly finds a painting of three clay pots. The highest pot is tilted to pour water into the pot below it, which overflows into the bottom pot. A Kenyan pastor once used this illustration to say that the first pot is like God, who pours into us – the second pot. Out of the overflow of what God has poured into us, we pour into others – the bottom pot. We must first be influenced by God before we can truly influence others to follow God.

In order to influence others as a Christian leader, you first need to be influenced by God. You need to receive the Living Water. You also need to learn from those God has given to influence you: parents, teachers, pastors, authors, and friends. As you are influenced, you can begin to influence others in the right direction.

If you truly are centred on God, learning and following his plan, you will naturally bring glory to his great name and you will bless humanity. You will overflow! In this book we will see how many young people in the Bible who were influenced by God influenced those in authority above them. Through them God accomplished his plans for his people and the nations. They influenced the course of history and blessed the whole world.

## INFLUENCING YOUR LEADERS

There are many leadership books about how to persuade or influence your followers, employees, church members, or children. These are for people who already have positions. Sometimes these books tell people how to get what they want in ways that seem manipulative and self-serving. But this book is about how followers who have no official position can influence their leaders.

Many people assume that you can only influence people younger than you or below you. In other words, influence moves from the top down, from leaders to their followers. But influence can move in both directions.[7] The employer and the employee can influence each other. The parent and the child both change each other. The majority and the minority will react to each other. Followers can influence their leaders. This book will teach you how.

The principles we will learn in this book are ones that we have seen work in our own lives. After I (Hankuri) learned some basic principles of influence, I saw another need for the church to intentionally mobilize her youth to get involved in global mission. I approached the coordinator of the Church Mission Committee, who then asked me to write a proposal explaining what it would entail. The proposal was approved by the church leadership and I was asked to make it happen. At the first conference, over 600 youth attended and over 100 were recruited to go as missionaries. Others committed to pray or give towards missions. Today, that conference is now an annual conference, and some of the participants from that first conference are missionaries and church elders. I am so humbled and grateful that God used me to not only influence my local congregation, but the top leadership of the church headquarters, and many unbelievers!

## WHAT TO EXPECT IN THIS BOOK

We will examine the lives of young people who influenced nations and leaders even when they did not have official positions of power. These influencers' stories are recorded in the Bible. Each young person faced a different challenge, similar to what we face today in our churches and nations. They were not primarily motivated by personal gain – although sometimes they were rewarded. They influenced a situation not for their own benefit, but for the good of others. Their actions led to great changes that were recorded forever in God's Word. The young "unofficial" leaders in the Bible will equip and encourage you, too, to step up and transform your nation and church.

This book is for anyone who feels helpless, who longs for a voice and an opportunity to help shape the direction of the church or society. You will learn these steps to becoming an influencer:

- Model the way.
- Inspire a shared vision.
- Challenge the process.
- Enable others to act.
- Encourage the heart.[8]

Once you learn these principles, you will no longer feel helpless and frustrated, but hopeful and energized.

We have seen how learning to be an influencer can make people feel empowered. In two countries where I (Phil) was training pastors and evangelists to be more effective in their ministries, I discussed solutions and made suggestions for bringing about change. They smiled sadly and said that those ideas wouldn't work. They were under the iron-fisted leadership of those who were above them in their denomination's hierarchical structure.

I began to share with them the ways in which they could be leaders without holding positions. They became excited and eagerly began to see how they could be an influencer in their own local situation. They found hope that they might begin to have a broader effect beyond their ministry. No longer defeated, now they were determined to make a change.

Together, we will discover how you, too, can make a change. You can be empowered to be an influencer wherever God has placed you. Influence makes ordinary people into world-changers. We begin by connecting with people in our daily lives, our family members, our communities, and our workplaces. Slowly, our influence can grow to the nations and the world. It took years for Gandhi's non-violent influence to win India's independence and for Nelson Mandela and his followers to bring down apartheid. So we must be prepared for a long journey and be patient as we seek to bring change. But influence has to start sometime. In fact, it starts right now, right where you are.

Influence starts right now, right where you are.

## QUESTIONS FOR DISCUSSION AND PERSONAL APPLICATION

1. Have you experienced the powerlessness and frustration Hankuri Gaya describes in his story? Share your story. What obstacles did you face when you tried to implement the changes you desired?

2. Think of an influencer who inspires you, whether someone famous or someone you know personally. If they have a title or a position, do you think that their title gave them their influence, or that their influence gave them their title?

3. What do you think of the definition of Christian leadership as "being influenced by God to become the person you are created to be, then influencing others to be become what God desires them to be"? How does this compare to other views of leadership?

CHAPTER ONE

# EARN THE RIGHT TO BE HEARD

To earn the right to be heard - you must listen, understand what matters most and assist people in some form or fashion.[9]

—— MARIA ELENA DURON ——

Students at the southern campus of Kaduna State University in Nigeria were not happy with the state government's decision to relocate one of their campuses to the northern part of the state. They gathered to protest, shouting and brandishing posters. When the vice chancellor of the university came to address them, the students only shouted louder. In the midst of this chaos, a lecturer, Prof Abbas Sodangi Ibrahim, simply raised his hands. All the students became quiet. This lecturer had invested a lot in mentoring students, so they listened. In front of the vice chancellor, he convinced them to shelve the protest and give room for dialogue.

In the introduction, we learned that influence is the ability to bring about change in another's beliefs, thoughts, actions, or behaviour. Influence cannot be forced or commanded but only earned. Influence made the students listen to a lecturer instead of the head of the university. Influence is demonstrated when people will listen to you, believe in the cause you are advocating, and begin to move in the direction you are encouraging them to go.

Before you have influence, you have to earn the right to be heard. This chapter will teach you how.

## BUILD A REPUTATION FOR TRUSTWORTHINESS

Influence will come as people trust you. Often leaders can be threatened by others below them who appear to have potential. They shouldn't be, but sometimes they are. It may be because they don't have as much education or drive, or because they don't have the ideas that the potential leader has.

Older people sometimes don't understand youth culture and this threatens them. People can also feel threatened by women or members of another tribe because they represent different groups. However, if they can trust you and your motives, then you can start to exercise influence.

Trust can take time to build, but it reaps wonderful results. You can develop trust by being dependable in character and faithful in your actions. Some people want to take the quick and easy way to the top, but there is no shortcut to the development and proof of one's character. There is no shortcut to faithfulness. You demonstrate character and faithfulness over time as you live them out in many different circumstances and situations. "Whoever can be trusted with very little can also be trusted with much" (Luke 16:10). As you are faithful over a period of time, you will begin to develop a growing influence within your sphere of life and ministry.

If you want to have influence with positional leaders, you need to have a reputation for being trustworthy. Your reputation will open the door for you to give thoughts and ideas to the decision-makers. The book of Proverbs makes this point several times:

> A good name is more desirable than great riches;
> to be esteemed is better than silver or gold
> (Proverbs 22:1).
>
> Do you see someone skilled in their work?
> They will serve before kings;
> they will not serve before officials of low rank
> (Proverbs 22:29).
>
> A faithful person will be richly blessed,
> but one eager to get rich will not go unpunished
> (Proverbs 28:20).

I (Hankuri) faced a challenge of acceptance when I reported as a new staff worker in Akure in the western part of Nigeria. I am from the north. Often the people from the western part of Nigeria don't see anything good coming from the north. They view us as educationally backward. So I worked hard. I got involved with students through training, writing reports and newsletters to stakeholders, pioneering a new campus fellowship, raising resources for the work, and providing leadership in hosting conferences. Six months later, one of the professors in a federal university introduced me to the chapel board where I was invited to preach. He said, "We have observed him. We can now trust him and what he can do." If your character is quality, be patient. With time and trust from others, your influence will grow.

## SUPPORT YOUR LEADER

Another way to build trust with people is to show that you are on their team. When someone suggests a new idea or a change, it is easy for leaders to be suspicious of that person's motives. They may be concerned that you are trying to lead people in a different direction or divert resources that they need for other tasks. They may wonder if you are just looking to get power and followers yourself. The best way to prevent this is to demonstrate to your leaders that you care about their priorities and want to help them accomplish their goals. Show this over a long period of time by making their work easier and serving them. You will gain their trust and earn more freedom to implement your own ideas.

Suppose your leader wants your team to do something that you see as outside of your organization's vision, mission, or strategic plan. This is common when new leaders come on board and their subordinates know the terrain better than they do. You might try speaking up and drawing attention to the difference between the leader's proposal and the organization's goals. However, if your leader is new or insecure, that person may see your action as trying to gain followers or shifting away from declared priorities.

To earn your leader's trust and prove that you have good motives, consider helping that leader to achieve what he or she sees as critical instead of contributing new ideas, as long as you can do it without compromising your core values. Rather than disengaging, what if you were to do more than assigned to show your support and commitment to the organization's goals? In the end, your leader might accept your ideas because you would have built trust by supporting your leader. Here are ways to show support to your leader to gain influence:

- Work hard and go the extra mile to accomplish the organization's and leader's goals.
- Be reliable.
- Provide good information to the leader.
- Identify potential problems or difficulties.
- Prevent problems instead of waiting for them to happen.
- Provide creative solutions.
- Defend and support the leader's (and organization's) decisions (if in line with biblical principles) whenever possible.
- Provide support and encouragement.
- Pray for them and with them.[10]

Each of these strategies can be used in the process of influence by those who have no official position and where there is no monetary cost to the influencer. However, by providing some of these, the person may earn the right to be heard and will then be able to have some influence in the issues that concern them.[11]

## NURTURE RELATIONSHIPS

Chigozie is the reason why many young people are still members at his church. He tells the children and teenagers stories, visits them in their homes, bonds with their families, and even gives them gifts. One day, a deacon gave one teenager the chore of arranging the chairs in the church as punishment for some wrongdoing. The offender decided he wasn't going to do it. But he met Chigozie's gaze when he was about to turn away. He reluctantly arranged the chairs, not because of the deacon, but because of Chigozie's influence.

You can probably think of times when someone gave you good advice but you ignored it because you didn't know the person well. On the other hand, there are probably times when someone close to you gave you a correction you didn't want to hear. Yet, because of the relationship, you took it to heart. Think about the people who have had the most influence upon your own life. Usually it will be those with whom you have a well-established relationship. Was it a parent? A spouse? A close friend or relative? This is the source of power in positive peer pressure. Peers influence others most strongly through relationship.

**We cannot influence without relationships.**

We can impact people at all different levels around us. Influence, and thus leadership, moves in many directions, and these directions usually flow along established relationship lines. In fact, we cannot influence without relationships. Bishop Desmond Tutu makes this point when he describes the Bantu concept of *ubuntu*: "*Ubuntu* speaks particularly about the fact that you can't exist as a human being in isolation . . . You are connected, and what you do affects the whole world. When you do well, it spreads out; it is for the whole of humanity."[12]

Your Circle of Influence

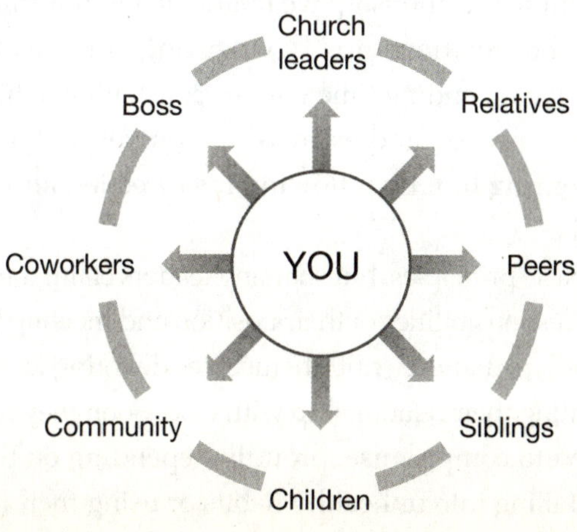

A person can have influence in all of the different relationships shown in the diagram. One can truly be a leader this way and yet not hold any official title or position. To be an influencer, carefully nurture and maintain good relationships with those within your circle.[13] As the apostle Paul puts it in Romans 12:18, "As far as it depends on you, live at peace with everyone." When you nurture relationships, you will begin to gain influence in your circle and even beyond. John Maxwell and Jim Dornan point out that, "When you help one person, you're really impacting a lot of other people. What you give to one person overflows into the lives of all the people that person impacts. *The nature of influence is to multiply*" (emphasis mine).[14]

Maintaining good relationships is not difficult, but it does require effort. Keep in touch with your friends through phone calls, messages, email, or writing, whether they reciprocate or not. Remember their birthdays and special days. Whenever possible, spend quality time with them. When you are together, learn to listen more to them rather than always doing the talking. Also try to open up about issues that affect you and seek their help. Look for ways to add value to their lives. Don't ask, "What can my friend do for me?" but rather, "What I can do for my friend?"

It is also crucial to nurture your relationship with God. Oswald Chambers writes: "The main thing about Christianity is not the work we do, but the relationship we maintain and the atmosphere produced by that relationship."[15] Nurturing your relationship with God involves spending time with him, listening to him speak in the Bible and prayer, and expressing yourself to him. It also involves honouring him by following his direction and obeying his commands.

These are basic principles, but so many leaders claim they are too busy with the responsibilities of their position and meeting the pressing needs of others that they find themselves devoting less and less time to cultivating their relationship with God. Soon they find themselves tempted to compromise, proudly depending on their own strength and falling into unhealthy habits or using their influence for selfish goals. As we mentioned in the introduction, to have a godly influence, it is crucial that you first be influenced by God.

Loving God and loving other people are the two greatest commandments, according to Jesus (Matthew 22:36-40). So perhaps it is not surprising that influence depends on good relationships with God and other people. Let's learn from an influencer in the Bible who did all he could to maintain his relationship with God and relationships with others.

## HOW JOSEPH EARNED AN AUDIENCE WITH THE KING

In Genesis 39–41, the Bible gives us an example of a young man who earned the right to be heard and became an influencer in every situation he encountered. Though he was unknown, eventually he gained a position where he could influence the fate of nations.

Joseph began in Egypt as a slave, a foreigner with no position and no power. But he faithfully fulfilled his responsibilities as a slave and he won the trust of his owner, Potiphar, the captain of the guard. He became the overseer of his house. Potiphar's wife attempted to seduce Joseph, but he refused to disobey God or to violate his master's trust. Unfortunately, she accused Joseph of attempting to rape her and Potiphar sent him to prison.

Again, Joseph had no power, and even less freedom than when he was a slave. But he remained faithful to the Lord and served him, winning the trust of the prison warden and being appointed over the prisoners. Wherever he went, Joseph built a reputation for being trustworthy. He demonstrated godly character in many situations over time. He supported his leader. Most of the time he earned influence as a result, but he obeyed God even when it cost him his influence. When he was falsely accused and imprisoned, he remained faithful to God instead of becoming discouraged and giving up.

Joseph also nurtured relationships by consistently adding value to others. He furthered the priorities of Potiphar and then the prison warden. In prison, he explained dreams to his fellow prisoners, including Pharaoh's butler. When the man was released, he forgot to advocate for Joseph to be released. How frustrating! Yet Joseph did not give up on adding value to others.

One day, which to Joseph was just like any other day in prison, he received a summons to appear before Pharaoh. When no one could interpret Pharaoh's troubling dream, the butler remembered that Joseph could interpret dreams. God revealed the meaning of the dream to Joseph so that he could explain it to Pharaoh: a terrible famine was coming, but first there would be years of abundance. In explaining Pharaoh's dreams and then proposing a plan, Joseph did not take the credit for himself. He faithfully gave God the praise.

Again, Joseph supported his leader by giving him advice that served Pharaoh's priorities. God enabled Joseph to come up with a plan: store up food in preparation for the famine. Pharaoh appointed Joseph second in command in the land. Joseph served Pharaoh and the people by organizing everyone in Egypt towards strategic preparation: building storehouses, reaping the harvest, and storing the surplus. Because God worked through Joseph, they survived.

Joseph didn't know what God had in store for him, but by remaining faithful and serving in whatever small way he could, he was in the right place at the right time to be used by God. Because he added value to others, the butler knew Joseph could help. Because he supported his leader and acted in trustworthy ways, he had already demonstrated ability to administer both Potiphar's household and the prison. Eventually, he administered the whole nation during a time of crisis and change.

By remaining faithful and serving in whatever small way he could, he was in the right place at the right time to be used by God.

Underlying all of this was the quality of faithfulness. Joseph's story illustrates what the master said to the faithful servants in Jesus' parable of the talents, "You have been faithful with a few things; I will put you in charge of many things" (Matthew 25:21b).

We who serve without position or power within the local church or our organizations must be faithful where we are and in what God has given us to do at the present time. We must support our leaders, nurture relationships, and build a reputation for being trustworthy. We must not compromise or give up when we face discouraging situations. Then, when the unexpected opportunity comes, we will be ready to step into new areas of influence.

## QUESTIONS FOR DISCUSSION AND PERSONAL APPLICATION

1. Who are the people in your circle of influence? Fill in the diagram below with your important relationships:

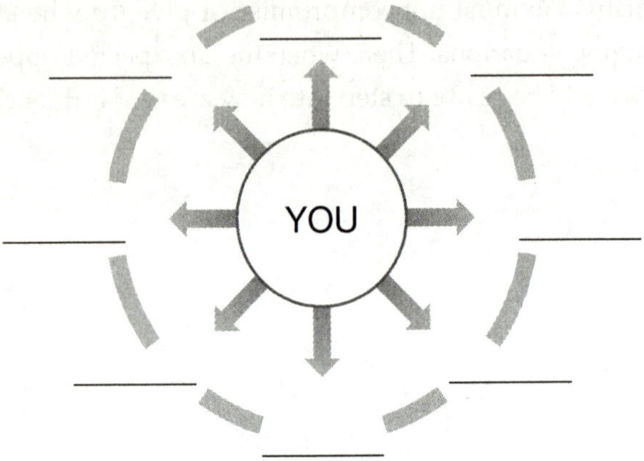


2. Think through what kind of influence you have on each person. Is it mostly relational, without any authority or formal position? Is it more positional, with some formal authority? Do you have positive influence or negative influence?

_______________________________________________

_______________________________________________

_______________________________________________

_______________________________________________

_______________________________________________

_______________________________________________

_______________________________________________

3. Since influence depends on relationship, what can you do to improve and strengthen the relationships you have with each person in your circle of influence?

4. What can you learn from Joseph about being faithful and trustworthy even in discouraging environments?

## CHAPTER TWO

# POWER AND INFLUENCE

**True leaders have power. This is not the power of position or wealth or title. It is more the power of influence, which can only be granted by those who chose to be followers.[16]**

**HYRUM SMITH**

Vimak has an ailment that makes him behave in a hostile manner. One day he and some other neighbourhood children were in the house together with his aunt. He locked the entrance to their house and kept the key in his pocket, refusing to open the door. His aunt, who was bigger in size than he, threatened him. So did the children's parents waiting outside, to no avail.

Finally, his childhood friend came to the scene. She greeted him and spoke to him in a soft manner. She reminded him of the unique qualities he possessed and how he was a good person. His countenance suddenly changed. He opened the door and gave her a hug.

This is the difference between the person with power and the one with influence. The aunt had power and authority, but the childhood friend succeeded in getting Vimak to open the door by using influence.

### INFLUENCE, NOT FORCE

We see many leaders using force, power, and position to compel others to do what they want accomplished. They may use their political leverage, military power, economic advantage, or spiritual authority to make people do what they want. Think of a politician's privileged advantage of speeding past others in the traffic, or a rich person giving a bribe to escape the punishment for breaking the law. Jesus describes how the rulers of the world lord it over their subjects because of power and position (Mark 10:42).

Even as Christians, it is easy for us to fall into the world's patterns. Daman was a young and vibrant Christian student on his campus who wanted to serve in student government. He promised to righteously serve the student body if he was elected, so the Christian students supported his campaign. The election was a stunning victory for Daman. Soon he forgot all the promises he had made when aspiring to the leadership position. He stopped attending fellowship meetings, giving the excuse that he was too busy with the responsibilities of his new position. As president of the student union government, Daman seized the opportunity to embezzle as much money as he could.

But the way of the world's power is not to be the way of the Christian. Jesus says, "Not so with you. Instead, whoever wants to be great among you must be your servant, and whoever wants to be first must be slave of all" (Mark 10:43-44). The servant leader cannot use force. Usually such leaders do not have institutional or positional power. They must influence hearts so their followers want to change their behaviour freely.[17] The way of the servant leader is the way of the Christian.

Servant leaders cannot use force. They must influence people's hearts so they want to change their behaviour freely.

Like Daman, Ajayi professed openly that he was a Christian. He became the chairman of his local government. But unlike Daman, he resisted his community's expectation to embezzle funds for them. After a few years, when Ajayi hadn't built a mansion or bought expensive cars, he was seen as a very foolish man who couldn't seize the opportunity to amass wealth for himself. He knew it was more important to build his heavenly mansions and be rewarded by the Lord for his faithful witness.

Even if you have a leadership position and power, influence produces more lasting and powerful change than force. Timothy Keller said in a sermon:

> If you seek power before service, you'll neither get power, nor serve. If you seek to serve people more than to gain power, you will not only serve people, you will gain influence. That's very much the way Jesus did it.[18]

It is better to refrain from using force and instead be a servant leader and influencer. In this chapter we will see how Jesus influenced the world by communicating his vision clearly to his disciples. We will see how your weakness and lack of power can actually be God's strength.

## POWER AND INFLUENCE

The New Testament redefines power in the life and ministry of the believer. Power is not based on physical, intellectual, social, economic, or political superiority. Instead power is expressed in service and weakness.

Jesus demonstrates this through his life. When we think of Jesus as an influencer, we might forget that he was not one of the successful people whose power came from his wealth, physical appearance, education, or status within society. Instead he was not very remarkable in the world's eyes. "He had no beauty or majesty to attract us to him . . . he was despised, and we held him in low esteem" (Isaiah 53:2-3).

Jesus was an ordinary man, a young carpenter, who had no position and no earthly power. He was an itinerant rabbi with an eclectic entourage composed of fishermen, tax gatherers, rebels against the state, and one who would eventually betray him. Yet no one can deny that Jesus was a true leader who exercised great influence. Jesus identified with us in weakness. He showed us that

God is in the ordinary. Jesus' mission involved making weakness strong. At the beginning of his ministry, he came to the synagogue in Nazareth and read from the prophet Isaiah:

> The Spirit of the Lord is on me,
> because he has anointed me
> to proclaim good news to the poor.
> He has sent me to proclaim freedom for the prisoners
> and recovery of sight for the blind,
> to set the oppressed free,
> to proclaim the year of the Lord's favour (Luke 4:18-19).

This was how he understood his divine calling. The Spirit of God was heavy upon him, giving an urgency to his ministry. This was a massive world wide mission. Jesus came in weakness to give the weak strength; in Christ the poor are made rich, the prisoners are set free, the blind are made to see, and the oppressed receive justice. Each one of these categories included both earthly and spiritual applications.

The way Jesus accomplished his mission was also one of influence rather than force. He could have displayed his divine power in terrifying lightning and earthquakes, in immediate judgement, or threats to repent and believe. Instead he selected 12 disciples. For three years he poured his life into them, teaching them, eating with them, and serving with them. He chose them "that they might be with him and that he might send them out to preach and to have authority to drive out demons" (Mark 3:14-15). He also commissioned them to make disciples of others. A. B. Bruce commends the training methodology Jesus used:

> The careful, painstaking education of the disciples secured that the Teacher's influence on the world should be permanent; that his kingdom should be founded on the rock of deep and indestructible convictions in the minds of the few, not on the

shifting sands of superficial evanescent [brief] impressions on the minds of the many.[19]

Jesus changed the world, not by force, but by influencing a few disciples. He communicated his vision clearly to them and empowered them to influence the world.

This is very different from the leadership we commonly see today. A person, government, or institution with authority will often impose changes from the top down without consulting the people that will be affected by the decision. When followers are told to obey, they are likely to resist the change. Once, I (Hankuri) changed the date of a student training event without consulting the student leaders responsible for implementing the event. Few students came or put their resources into making it succeed. Afterwards, one of the student leaders said to me, "Uncle, we decided to do it your way. I hope you have achieved what you wanted." I learnt my lesson the hard way. As Spencer Johnson writes, "a change imposed is a change opposed."[20]

Jesus showed us a new model. He inspired people so they caught his passion, involved them so they learned and were equipped, and finally handed over the task to these followers. You, too, can cast the vision and communicate clearly the benefits of your desired outcome so that people buy in to that direction. You can involve people who will be affected by the change in the decision-making. Give them the opportunity to share their thoughts and ideas, to ask questions, and provide possible solutions. They will be more supportive and feel ownership of the proposed changes.

Jesus started with a small band of men who were trained and sent forth to the ends of the earth. His disciples, and then many others, got involved in planting the church across the known world. They eventually brought change as the gospel spread throughout the whole Roman Empire. Even unbelievers saw that these disciples had "turned the world upside down" (Acts 17:6 KJV). The global change continues even up to today, centuries later.

Jesus had lasting influence beyond his short ministry upon earth. This encourages us as we seek to bring about lasting change. Influence may not reap fast and dramatic results. It may look like weakness and foolishness. But we are not living only for ourselves and our generation. We have a long view of our divine calling here on earth and we know God's power is at work.[21]

> **Influence may not reap fast and dramatic results, but we are not living only for ourselves and our generation.**

## PAUL

Paul was influenced by Jesus to see power in weakness. The world's system views God's way of salvation and the Christian way of life as "foolishness" and "weakness". Christ's work on the cross looks like the foolishness and weakness of God: "For the foolishness of God is wiser than human wisdom, and the weakness of God is stronger than human strength" (1 Corinthians 1:25).

But this should make us rejoice. Because God chooses to use weakness and turn it into strength, he chooses to use us! Paul continues:

> Brothers and sisters, *think of what you were when you were called.* Not many of you were wise by human standards; not many were influential; not many were of noble birth. But God chose the foolish things of the world to shame the wise; God chose the weak things of the world to shame the strong. He chose the lowly things of this world and the despised things – and the things that are not – to nullify the things that are, so that no one may boast before him (1 Corinthians 1:26-29, emphasis mine).

Most of us can identify with this description. As we look at these people and realize that this is who we are, we come to the marvellous conclusion that we are the kind of people that God desires and plans to use to bring about his purposes! Our inadequacies may in fact be exactly what God wants to use to show his ability more greatly.

Achonye showed up for an acting audition, but the judges told him they were looking for university graduates, and he had no formal education. They refused to listen to him or see his performance. A few years later, Achonye has become a major director in the movie industry. He now has the ability to influence aspiring talent and mentor them to be godly performers. Perhaps if he had been chosen to become an actor, he would have danced to the tune of the ungodliness that has overshadowed the industry.

Our weakness can actually be the very thing God wants to use to display his power! Not being in a position or having resources today may be your opportunity to give God even more glory. If anyone asks you about your age or qualifications to make you feel inadequate, remember that it is God who has called you to touch lives just the way you are. What we see as a disadvantage may be an asset God has entrusted into our hands. The challenge for us influencers is to embrace God's foolishness and weakness, the power of our lives. Paul is a wonderful example:

> Three times I pleaded with the Lord to take [the thorn in my flesh] away from me. But [Jesus] said to me, "My grace is sufficient for you, for my power is made perfect in weakness." Therefore I will boast all the more gladly about my weaknesses, so that Christ's power may rest on me. That is why, for Christ's sake, I delight in weaknesses, in insults, in hardships, in persecutions, in difficulties. For when I am weak, then I am strong (2 Corinthians 12:8-10).

Michael Gorman comments:

> For Paul what matters is that *his* weakness allows *God's power* to be manifested. [This] power means that no one can attribute the effects of Paul's preaching and teaching to successful marketing techniques – ancient or modern – but only to the inherent power of the cross as the revelation of God [emphasis his].[22]

This is especially relevant to those of us who have no position. God's grace is sufficient to fulfil his calling in our lives from out of our weakness or lack of position. As we serve others, we will completely depend upon God's power because we know that we do not have any power ourselves. Then only God will get the glory because everyone will know the power does not come from us.

## INFLUENCING FROM VULNERABILITY AND WEAKNESS

Miriam had been physically and sexually abused by her uncle since she was nine years old. She was ashamed to talk about the pain that lingered in her heart. While in university, she encountered Christ and everything about her changed. Though it felt awkward at first, she decided to share her story and how God had helped her. Her story attracted ladies to her who had experienced similar situations, and she saw the importance of her boldness. She eventually began a movement that advocates to protect girls. God's power has been at work even in her pain.

We see another amazing story of God's power obviously at work in weakness in the life of the Samaritan woman in John 4. Jesus sat beside a well and saw a woman coming to draw water. He asked her for a drink. In his weakness and thirst, he began the most powerful conversation that woman would ever experience.

Her weakness was obvious. She was a Samaritan, a group that the Jews despised. As a woman, she should not have been talking to a strange man. In the conversation it also becomes clear that she had a bad reputation. She had had five husbands and was living with a man she was not married to. She probably went to draw water from the well at noon because none of the other women would be there at that time.

This woman's weakness made her aware of the spiritual need which Jesus offered to fill. She realized that Jesus was no ordinary man but the Messiah! She ran back to the village and said, "Come, see a man who told me everything I ever did. Could this be the Messiah?" (John 4:29).

The Samaritan woman's weakness made her testimony even more powerful. She had been hiding from the others in the village. Now she returned to the village and openly acknowledged her past that she had been trying to avoid. If she had gone and said, "Come see the Messiah!" they probably would have laughed at her and ignored her invitation. However, by being open and vulnerable, the people of her village found her to be credible. The villagers must have wondered what experience could have convinced her to publicly admit to her failings with such frankness. Her vulnerability and weakness influenced them to see Jesus for themselves.

Jesus ended up staying there two more days because the villagers wanted to hear from him. "And because of his words many more became believers. They said to the woman, 'We no longer believe just because of what you said; now we have heard for ourselves'" (John 4:41-42).

Being an influencer is about serving, even if it means giving up power to empower others.

The Samaritan woman's story teaches us that Christ does not need you to look holy and perfect for him to use you.

Encountering Jesus can transform the weakest person into an influencer. For instance, Patrobas was notorious in his missionary kids' college for breaking the rules. On one occasion, he and a group of boys even stole a goat, slaughtered it, and roasted the meat on the rocks. Then in his final year at the college he had an encounter with Jesus Christ that turned the story of his life around. He became a radical follower of Jesus Christ. Today he is serving the Lord as a missionary. His decision and the change in his life also influenced his younger brother to trust Jesus Christ.

Being an influencer is not about lust for power and authority. It is not about being a big boss, getting your way, and being able to force others to do what you want. Being an influencer is about serving, even if it means giving up power to empower others. Because God's power is made perfect in weakness, your age, position, or gender should not prevent you from influencing others. God can deploy what seems to you like weakness or disadvantages to change the world for his glory.

## QUESTIONS FOR DISCUSSION AND PERSONAL APPLICATION

1. Do you ever doubt yourself and think you cannot be a leader because you are just an ordinary person? Knowing that Jesus was an ordinary person, how does this affect your thinking about becoming an influencer? Explain.

2. As Robert Coleman says, "One must decide where he wants his ministry to count - in the momentary applause of popular recognition or in the reproduction of his life in a few chosen men who will carry on his work after he has gone. Really it is a question of which generation we are living for."[23] Examine your own motives for wanting to be an influencer. Is it for the crowd's applause today or for building up the kingdom of God by influencing others for the future?

3. Honestly think about the methods you have pursued in the past. Were you aiming at power and authority or were you pursuing humble service? Explain a time you did one or the other. What was the result?

## CHAPTER THREE

# WHAT DOES AN INFLUENCER DO?

**The purpose of leadership is to find ways to channel the initiatives of the membership into constructive avenues so that the body is edified . . . We need men and women who are able to inspire their brethren to cooperate in a spiritual way to do the work of Jesus Christ.[24]**

**——— GOTTFRIED OSEI-MENSAH ———**

In secondary school, Dirmicit learned how to perform personal checks for breast cancer. She helped her mother discover a lump in her breast. Unfortunately the cancerous lump was detected too late, and her mother passed away.

Eight years later, Dirmicit was a university student and she had been learning about cancer. With the support of her campus fellowship and mentors, she launched an online campaign educating women on how to detect breast cancer early. Her peers joined in.

Finally, she organized a community-based campaign in a rural area, working with women who were leaders in the market and worship centres. Two National House of Representative members from her community and several other leading figures were attracted to her campaign. The campaign reached 250 women and trained 79 how to examine themselves.

Dirmicit faced a challenge that brought her to the point of taking action and influencing others. This now leads us to ask: If you see an opportunity for influence, how do you actually begin to change the situation? What does an influencer do?

In the book, *The Leadership Challenge*, James M. Kouzes and Barry Z. Posner describe the five characteristics of an effective leader, which apply equally to influencers without title or position. John Deisher helpfully recasts these leadership characteristics as follows:[25]

1. Influencers **model the way** by setting standards of excellence and achieving small wins.
2. Influencers **enable others to act** by fostering collaboration and strengthening others.
3. Influencers **challenge the process**, searching for opportunities, experimenting, and taking risks.
4. Influencers **encourage the heart**, recognizing contributions and celebrating accomplishments.
5. Influencers **inspire a shared vision**, envisioning the future and enlisting others.

In this chapter we will identify these five characteristics in the life of Jonathan. He is a powerful example of what an influencer does.

## MODEL THE WAY (1 SAMUEL 13:1–14:14)

Jonathan was the son of King Saul of Israel. He was a prince and a commander in Israel's army. But he was not the king and so he had no ultimate decision-making authority.

> Influencers model the way by setting standards of excellence and achieving small wins.

The Philistines continually oppressed the nation of Israel. In order to free his nation from bondage, Jonathan led 1,000 soldiers under his command against the enemy and defeated a Philistine outpost. [26] In response, the Philistines invaded Israel with soldiers as numerous as the sands on the seashore to crush this little rebellion (1 Samuel 13:5). King Saul was immobilized with fear and retreated with his army. Frightened soldiers deserted. It is at this point that we see Jonathan influence the affairs of the nation as a true leader.

The nation faced a serious emergency situation and needed to be defended and protected. Jonathan responded using "The Pattern of Proactive Influence", which we will discuss more in the next chapter. Jonathan was triggered to fight for a **cause**. He could not remain idle. With great faith, he took **action** to liberate his people.

In 1 Samuel 14:1-23, Jonathan decided to start a fight with the Philistines to model the way for everyone around him.

Jonathan's Pattern of Proactive Influence

First, he **involved** his young armour bearer (1 Samuel 14:6). Jonathan wouldn't have had a team if he had not been able to influence this young man. Jonathan told him: "Come, let's go over to the outpost of those uncircumcised men. Perhaps the Lord will act in our behalf. Nothing can hinder the Lord from saving, whether by many or few" (1 Samuel 14:6).

Some might have felt hopeless in the face of the vast Philistine force. Marshal Ferdinand Foch, the French World War I hero, said, "There are no hopeless situations; there are only men and women who have grown hopeless about them."[27]

But Jonathan believed in a great God. His faith that God could deliver gave him confidence to move forward and challenge the enemy. I am struck by the word he used: *perhaps*. There is a *perhaps* of doubt, and there is a *perhaps* of faith! The *perhaps* of doubt is that we are not sure if something is going to happen or not. We might say, "Perhaps it will rain today." We use *perhaps* because we are not sure. It might rain and it might not.

But the *perhaps* of faith is different. The *perhaps* of faith is trust in God's power to act in our impossible circumstances according to his will. The *perhaps* of faith is the confidence that if God wills something to happen it doesn't matter if we are many or few, it will take place. This *perhaps* of faith leads to hope even in the most desperate situations.

I believe we see the *perhaps* of faith displayed in Jonathan's life. The enemy's threat was overwhelming and Jonathan's resources were almost non-existent. To make matters worse, they would have to climb a cliff before engaging the enemy, who could attack them from the top as they climbed. But Jonathan said, "Nothing can hinder the Lord from saving, whether by many or by few."

He then proceeded to lay out a test to see if it was *perhaps* God's will for them to attack this vastly superior force. This is seen in 1 Samuel 14:8-10:

> Jonathan said, "Come, then; we will cross over toward them and let them see us. If they say to us, 'Wait there until we come to you,' we will stay where we are and not go up to them. But if they say, 'Come up to us,' we will climb up, because that will be our sign that the Lord has given them into our hands."

They did this and the Philistines mocked them, telling them to come up. So, Jonathan and his armour bearer went into the pass, climbed the cliffs, engaged the Philistines in battle, and killed 20 of them. By faith these two took courageous action because of their cause. They defeated the Philistines – a real act of faith! Then look at what God does, described in verses 15-16: "Then panic struck the whole army – those in the camp and field, and those in the outposts and raiding parties – and the ground shook. It was a panic sent by God. Saul's lookouts at Gibeah in Benjamin saw the army melting away in all directions." The ground shook, probably as the result of an earthquake, and panic set in. These were things only God could do!

Jonathan's Circle of Influence

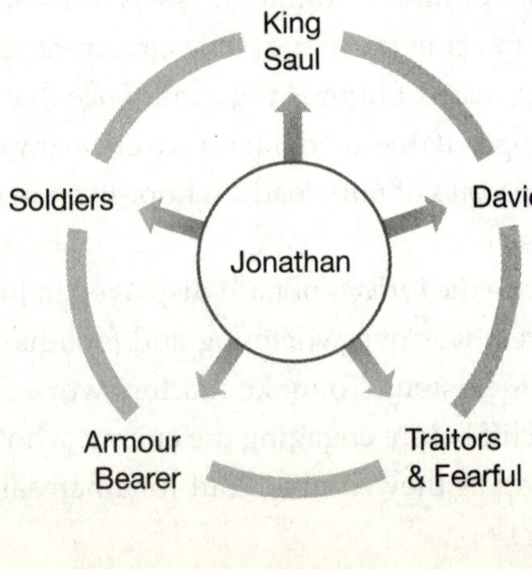

King Saul was sitting around with his small army. Finally, he figured out something was happening. He assembled his men for battle. By starting the battle, Jonathan influenced Saul, the leader in the highest position, to action. And therefore, he also influenced the soldiers to be involved. Then, the traitors who had joined with the Philistines, the deserters, and the fearful soldiers who had hidden themselves came back to the army. These people all got **involved** because Jonathan acted. This shows the power of one ordinary man to influence the people at the top, his peers, and those under his leadership.

Jonathan used the pattern of proactive influence to bring **change**. Through the actions of a young influencer, the people of Israel were delivered from the bondage and oppression of the Philistines.

The enemy was huge; the human resources were small. But Jonathan modelled the way to deal with an outside threat and set the standard for bravery, strategy, and action. Jonathan's faith and action eventually influenced all of Israel's army to defeat the Philistines. Jonathan's victory over 20 men was a small win, but God turned it into a major victory for Israel. Kouzes and Posner write:

> [Leaders'] deeds are far more important than their words when determining how serious they really are about what they say. Words and deeds must be consistent. Exemplary leaders go first. They go first by setting the example through daily actions that demonstrate they are already committed to their beliefs.[28]

Like Jonathan, a young man in Nigeria identified a problem and modelled the way for change. Lengdung saw the rottenness in his Jenta community and Nigeria at large. Reading the Bible and other books had helped Lengdung when he was grieving the loss of his mother and younger sibling. So he and his friends from church decided to provide books to change the mindset of young people in their community. Today, they run a community library in Jenta, which has also sparked action to address problems in the community. Lengdung also leads discussions of books and societal issues on a social media platform called Book-Troverts. One thing you cannot take away from Lengdung is his passion for learning and books. If you happen to run into him in a bookshop in Jos, you'll find he does not only talk about transforming his community, he leads the way in transforming himself and inspiring others to do the same.

To be an influencer, you need to be a person of integrity. Whatever position you have or do not have, be sure to model consistent words and deeds. Your character will give you credibility so others will trust you and follow your lead. Set an example through your daily lifestyle and attitude. Inspire people with your faith in action. God can use your small wins to influence many people through you.

As you look at your own life, ask yourself:

- Am I living by and applying high standards of excellence?
- Am I diligent? Am I trustworthy?
- Have I been faithful in small things so that I have established a record of achievement and accomplishment of my goals?

## ENABLE OTHERS TO ACT (1 SAMUEL 18:3)

After David defeated Goliath and God gave Israel the victory, Jonathan took David under his wing. He became David's biggest supporter and champion. He fostered collaboration. His spirit became one with David's. He made a covenant with David and loved David as himself.

> Influencers enable others to act by fostering collaboration and strengthening others.

Jonathan also strengthened David by giving him his tunic, his sword, his bow, and his belt. Swords were rare and valuable. The Philistines had outlawed blacksmiths among the Israelites, so only King Saul and Jonathan had a sword and spear (1 Samuel 13:22). This was a remarkable act of empowerment. Because Jonathan enabled and strengthened him, David was victorious: "The Philistine commanders continued to go out to battle, and as often as they did, David met with more success than the rest of Saul's officers, and his name became well-known" (1 Samuel 18:30). Without a sword David could not have led the Israelites in battle against the Philistines.

Influencers add value to other people's lives. It can be materially, as in providing a weapon, tools, resources, or relevant information. It can be emotional support and commitment to the other person, such as visiting, giving verbal encouragement, or joining the project at hand. We see all three of these in Jonathan's enabling and strengthening of David.

Lengdung, too, empowered someone to act. He has influenced Philemon Jidontok, who was in a book club he led. Lengdung mentors him and provides him with e-books, enabling Jidontok to lead a new book club in northern Nigeria.

As you seek to be an influencer, you must ask yourself, how can I add value to the people that I want to influence? Consider also the people you want to involve in the change process. Rather than thinking of them as followers, think of them as partners. They have gifts and abilities and can help share the burden of leadership. Ask yourself:

- Who can I strengthen in their faith to step out and do great things for God?
- How can I empower them to be what God wants them to be?
- How can I help them to use their gifts and abilities to accomplish God's purpose for their lives?

These questions are not manipulative if our true desire is to see others succeed and to see the kingdom of God built.

## CHALLENGE THE PROCESS (1 SAMUEL 19:1-7; 20:32 FF.)

Jonathan challenged the process or the status quo to protect David. In 1 Samuel 19, King Saul ordered Jonathan and those in his court to kill David. Jonathan challenged the process. First, he warned David of the plot against him.

Then Jonathan went to King Saul and gave logical evidence why he should not pursue this course of action. He listed all of David's

> **Influencers challenge the process, searching for opportunities, experimenting, and taking risks.**

accomplishments and victories on behalf of the nation of Israel and how Saul had personally benefitted through David's service. He reminded Saul how glad he had been when the Lord brought victory over the Philistines through David's defeat of Goliath. Jonathan also appealed to King Saul's sense of right and wrong, "Why then would you do wrong to an innocent man like David by killing him for no reason?" (1 Samuel 19:5c).

Saul agreed not to kill David. For a short time, Jonathan's influence protected David and brought about a change in Saul's view and treatment of him.

Providing evidence is an effective way to influence those who are in positions of authority. It can be a listing of evidence as Jonathan did to influence his father's opinion of David, or it can be providing experiential evidence as we will see later in the life of Daniel. All leaders want progress, but they are careful of wasting resources or causing more problems than they solve. When confronted with firm facts and other kinds of evidence it can be hard for leaders not to begin the process of changing their ideas.

Selya Blessing Nanyak convinced her leader with evidence. As leader of the female students of a campus ministry, she wanted to host a conference to holistically empower ladies to be godly, productive women who contribute to society. She and her team presented a written proposal to her leader, stating the reason for holding the event, how they were going to raise funds, the skills they were going to teach during the programme, and how they were going to mobilize the female students to attend the event. She also shared her experience hosting events and showed images of different products her friends could teach women to make. The evidence convinced her leader to agree to her proposal. Over 100 participants attended the first conference. It was so well received that the conference became a national event held in each region in Nigeria, with tracks added for young men.

Back to David's story. Unfortunately, Saul changed his mind and tried again to kill David. When David was concerned that his life was in danger, he decided not to show up at the king's table for the new moon festival Saul was hosting. Saul's response would show whether he wanted to kill him or not. Jonathan agreed to David's plan, though it put him at risk.

When Saul asked Jonathan where David was, Jonathan gave an excuse for David. Saul became very angry at Jonathan and revealed his intent to kill David. But Jonathan said, "Why should he be put to death? What has he done?" (1 Samuel 20:32). Then Saul threw his javelin at Jonathan! Jonathan had taken a great risk in challenging the process!

Challenging the process can be risky. MaryKate Morse gives this insight on risk as one challenges the process, serves, and seeks to protect others:

> People take risks in planting a new church, starting a creative social program, moving overseas to be neighbours with strangers, or opening a new business . . . Jesus often took risks, whether healing on the Sabbath or challenging the Pharisees' motive for tithing . . . People who are averse to taking risks rarely say or do anything to rock the boat. Risk-avoiders prefer the status quo out of fear that things might go terribly wrong. Risk-takers generally have more . . . influence.[29]

We need courage and wisdom to challenge the process. Like King Saul, leaders may feel we are challenging their leadership or authority, not simply their method of doing things. This is because leaders often have invested a lot of their life in establishing and developing the process that now is being challenged. We may face their anger and opposition in some cases, but we must count the cost if we want to be an influence for change.

At the same time, we should avoid unnecessary offence. Though the word *challenge* may sound aggressive, it will be in your best interest to avoid confronting or threatening your leader. Instead, emphasize that you are simply searching for opportunities to do things better. As much as possible, show your leader that you are on the same team, trying to help accomplish the desired goals. Think strategically about the fears of your leader, connect with that person's passion, or seek to share your new idea with people whose opinion your leader respects.

Sometimes in our contexts, we feel we need to challenge not just the process that an individual leader is suggesting, but a way of life upheld by a whole community. For instance, a young Tanzanian pastor moved to a new village church. When he and his wife returned from the field, the husband carried the firewood while his wife carried the maize. For a man to carry firewood was unheard of in that culture – that was women's work. The villagers mocked his manhood using a local expression: "Your wife is sitting on you!" However, the young husband persisted.

Later, some people from the village passed by his house and heard laughter. They asked him, "Why are you always laughing at your house? We heard you having a great time." The villagers were surprised that the couple would be so happy. The young pastor's influence and respect in the community grew as they realized his new ideas had brought happiness in his marriage.

## ENCOURAGE THE HEART (1 SAMUEL 23:16)

David knew he was destined to be the next ruler of Israel. Saul was jealous of him because he could see the Holy Spirit upon David, no longer upon himself. So, King Saul hunted David to try to kill him. David was discouraged, in danger, and uncertain.

Jonathan sought out David in the desert, encouraged his heart "and helped him find strength in God" (1 Samuel 23:16). These were not empty words. We saw in Jonathan's clifftop battle with the Philistines how he had a living faith in God's power. He had proven God to be trustworthy and able to deliver even in seemingly impossible circumstances. As an influencer, he led David into a deepened sense of trust and dependence upon God. Jonathan had credibility because he had lived it out and demonstrated the faithfulness of God.

> Influencers encourage the heart, recognizing contributions, and celebrating accomplishments.

Encouragement spurs those who are working to do more and those who are not to start serving faithfully and giving their best. When you encourage your partners, they will remain engaged with you and work to fulfil the vision you have shared with them. As you think about becoming an influencer, ask yourself:

- Do I encourage others?
- Am I able to see who is making contributions towards the goal? Do I recognize and honour their contribution?
- Do I celebrate small wins as we take steps to accomplish our goal and to achieve change?

Some concrete ways you can encourage other people include verbally appreciating team members, whether privately or before the entire team, and writing them notes of affirmation. You can commemorate special days or accomplishments by buying small gifts, taking people out for a meal to celebrate a special day or an accomplishment, or hosting a party to celebrate milestones. Other people may feel empowered if you point out helpful resources, give them credit for their accomplishments and opportunities to present them to leadership or colleagues, and invest in their professional development through training events or more one-on-one time with leaders.

## INSPIRE A SHARED VISION (1 SAMUEL 23:15–17 FF.)

Jonathan inspired David when he found him in the desert. He envisioned the future: "'Don't be afraid,' he said. 'My father Saul will not lay a hand on you. You will be king over Israel, and I will be second to you'" (1 Samuel 23:17).

By rights, Jonathan should have been the next king, but he was in tune with God's plan. By now he probably knew that the prophet

> Influencers inspire a shared vision, envisioning the future and enlisting others.

Samuel had anointed David to be the next king. As a result, Jonathan made God's plan for David his own vision. He encouraged David by reminding him of that vision, even though he knew he would only be second to David in the kingdom. Jonathan gave a bold and exciting view of what life would be like for the two of them. Later he unselfishly used his influence in the life of David to make this a reality.

A shared vision changes a relationship. As established leaders share their vision, they can move others from being followers to fellow workers. Through a shared vision, influencers who have no official position can move the established leader to the status of a fellow worker even if that person's official position does not change. Jonathan was willing to move from the position of a leader to that of a follower for their shared vision to become a reality. This was only possible because of the relationship that the two men had developed over the years. A shared vision requires a relationship between the influencer and the one being influenced to succeed.

For a shared vision to inspire and influence others to join us, four key factors must be in place: clarity, commitment, communication, and completion.

### Clarity

First, we must be clear on the vision ourselves. A vision is our view of what we want to see happen, to accomplish, or to change in the future. It is our ideal state, our destination. Sometimes people want to be leaders or want things to be changed but they don't have a clear idea of where they are going or how to get there.

The story is told of a youth who went on a journey and came to a place where the road branched in two directions. He asked an old man who was standing there, "Which road should I take?"

"Where do you want to go?" responded the old man.

"I don't know," the young man answered.

To which the old man said, "Then it doesn't matter."[30]

If we do not have a clear vision of the future, if we have no focus and are aimlessly drifting along, no one will even know if we end up at our destination. Faustin Ntamushobora writes, "Sometimes leaders want to do everything and they lose focus . . . Without focus no impact is made and less is achieved."[31]

No one will be influenced to follow us if they have no idea what their final goal or destination will be. They will ask, "Where are you taking us? Is it something we can be excited about and enthusiastically support?" But if we are not clear on where we are going, we can be sure that not many people will be influenced to join us on the journey. Cohen and Bradford write, "A powerful vision paints a graphic picture of how its successful accomplishment changes the lives of some important group(s). It isn't just *what* will occur, but *why* it's important."[32]

### Commitment

It is not enough for us to be clear about the vision. We must be willing to be committed to it. Any vision that we are not committed to wholeheartedly will never attract others. Paint a picture of the vision with words, but pave the way for the vision with action.

Have you heard the story about the pig and the chicken? It was time for an event in their master's house that required pork and an egg sauce. The chicken complained to the pig that they were going to take away all her eggs. The pig looked at the chicken and said, "Your lot is better. Mine is a total commitment!" Many of us are like the chicken that contributes only an egg towards the vision but complains the most. We must be ready for total commitment like the pig if we are going to inspire people to follow our vision.

We can see the need for this kind of vision from the example of Kenya's Christians for a Just Society:

> We can ask ourselves the question: what should we aim at? It is tempting to aim at some "maximalist" set of economic

> targets that seek to uplift the bottom half of society to higher than subsistence levels of existence. Will such a vision, however, release the passion and creative energy of a people? To achieve real change within the span of one generation we must have a vision that seeks to transform our society [such as] the achievement of each person's full potential (spiritually, mentally, socially and physically) within the context of a just community / nation.[33]

If our vision is simply something that might be nice to have sometime, but we are not wholeheartedly dedicated to achieving our desired future, we will not inspire others to share the journey with us in fulfilling the vision. We need passion and commitment to the vision to influence others.

### Communication

We must communicate the vision and the plan to achieve it to others and bring them on board. A shared vision must be communicated to others, or it will simply remain a hidden desire within us – a private and personal vision. That may not necessarily be wrong, but it will not bring about transformational change within our church or organization.

We must also communicate the plan for how we will accomplish that vision. Vision is the future desired state, the change we want to accomplish. It is our final destination. But we need a plan for how to move towards the destination if we want to arrive.

### Completion

Finally, we must complete the work. Inspiration of a shared vision is nothing unless we influence others to do what is necessary to actually work it out. Often in churches or other organizations there can be a lot of enthusiastic talk that stirs up an emotional response, but people don't execute the steps to fulfil that shared vision. Larry Bossidy and Ram Charan say:

> Execution is *the* great unaddressed issue in the business world today. Its absence is the single biggest obstacle to success and the cause of most of the disappointments that are mistakenly attributed to other causes (emphasis theirs).[34]

This could very easily be applied to the church and many Christian organizations today.

I (Phil) was in a large group some years ago and we decided to form a committee to discuss an issue that would affect us all. After the decision to form the committee, the chairperson was ready to move on to the next item on the agenda. But no one had been assigned to convene such a committee. I raised my hand and pointed out that if we didn't appoint a convener, we would come back the following year and nothing would have been done. The group had an agreed purpose, but we would have utterly failed to accomplish it, because there would have been no execution.

When we inspire a shared vision, we also must put the mechanisms in place that will ensure that we accomplish our purpose. Think about what you would like to change in your church, job, school, organization, or your country. Ask yourself:

- Do I have a vision that will motivate others to join with me?
- How can I communicate a clear picture of the change I hope for?
- How will this change make a different and better future?

The five principles we have covered in this chapter, embodied in Jonathan, show us what an influencer does. Now that you know what influencers do, it is time for you to step out and do the same. Remember, the greatest farmer in the community is not the man who clears the farm or plants the highest quantity of seed. It is the man who daily invests time in weeding, tending, and doing whatever it takes to ensure that he has a good yield at the time of harvest. Are you ready to invest in becoming an influencer?

Jonathan and David are no longer on the stage. Mandela of

South Africa, Kenyatta of Kenya, Chinua Achebe of Nigeria, and other great leaders of Africa have done their part. Now it is your time to influence others. It is time for you to arise and model the way, enable others, challenge the process, encourage the heart, and inspire a shared vision. As you take action, God can use you to transform the world and honour him.

It is your time to influence others. It is time for you to arise.

## QUESTIONS FOR DISCUSSION AND PERSONAL APPLICATION

1. As you look at your circle of influence, can you identify ways in which you are modelling the way for positive change and growth with each relationship?

2. What is your "inspiring vision" that you can share with others in such a way that they will want to join you in making a difference for your home, church, community, and country?

3. Who within your circle of influence needs someone to come alongside of them to protect them from the processes of life that can sometimes be so harmful and destructive?

4. Within your circle of influence who needs empowering? Who can you enable to become more than they already are? To whom can you add value, by giving them skills or access to resources to help them become more valuable members of society?

_______________________________________________
_______________________________________________
_______________________________________________
_______________________________________________
_______________________________________________
_______________________________________________
_______________________________________________

5. Who within your circle of influence needs encouragement and affirmation? List specifically how you could strengthen this person through acts of appreciation. How do you plan to give this gift of encouragement and affirmation to them?

_______________________________________________
_______________________________________________
_______________________________________________
_______________________________________________
_______________________________________________
_______________________________________________
_______________________________________________

CHAPTER FOUR

# HOW TO BEGIN TO INFLUENCE

**If there will be any lasting change in social, economic, and political settings of the African nations . . . the leaders must be ready for total transformation. We must be willing to recognise that we do have a problem, identify it, and deal with it. In essence, we need a solution that will have material results.[35]**

**— IBRAHIM OMONDI —**

Reactive people ignore problems. They sit on the sidelines and watch things happen, then ask, "How did we get here?" Only after the crisis has begun do they try to figure out how to respond.

For instance, leaders in a community in north-eastern Nigeria saw the growing rate of drug abuse in their community and how it was destroying the youth. They lured the youth into a meeting and then invited drug enforcement agents to arrest the youth. Instead of curbing the problem, drug abuse escalated. The youth are now hostile and resistant to assistance from anyone.

In contrast, an influencer is proactive. Influencers don't ask, "What happened?" They make things happen. Influencers see a problem beginning to develop and they decide to take action. Even when they do not hold an official position, they use their relationships to bring about change.

Godiya Lumi decided to tackle the same problem of drug abuse in the same region of Nigeria. Godiya is a gifted musician and producer who has had opportunities to train abroad. He could have made money in Nigeria's big cities, but he chose to set up his studio in his village. He noticed the community's high rate of drug addiction and felt God moving him to do something. He wrote personal letters inviting young addicts for a meeting. He invited those who showed up to join a Bible study and recovery programme. To his amazement, over half the people who received his letters came for the Bible study, including drug dealers and distributors. Several have completely recovered, and the young people formerly seen as a nuisance have formed a drama and music team! Godiya has also empowered some of them with seed capital for small businesses. One of them invested in farming and his investment grew four times.

Once you have earned the right to be heard and gained influence, it is time to use that influence. In this chapter, we will talk about what might spark you to be a proactive influencer like Godiya in your community. Perhaps you are asking: What kinds of problems should I notice? How should I decide where to exercise influence? What causes would be worthy of moving me into action?

Let's look at the "Pattern of Proactive Influence". As the last chapter mentioned briefly, this is the pattern you can use in your setting to become a leader, just as leaders in the Bible did.

The Pattern of Proactive Influence

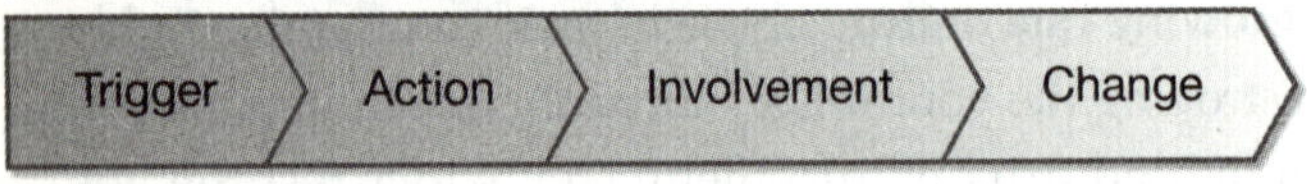


## THE PATTERN OF PROACTIVE INFLUENCE

The pattern starts with some kind of **trigger**. Just as someone pulls a trigger to shoot a bullet from a gun, so certain situations are like pulling a trigger that motivates a person to begin to influence others. Once people are aware of a situation, a problem, a challenge, or a need for change, they become so convinced that they move into action. They can't sit idly by or wait on the sidelines. They can't remain spectators and watch things continue to go wrong or evil to persist when they could solve the problem in a better and more effective way.

The second part of the pattern is **action**. Moved by a need for change, the influencer starts to do something to correct the situation, to resolve the issue, and to relieve the suffering. Because influencers are proactive, they often begin to act even before others (including official leadership) see or feel the need to do something.

This, then, leads us to the third step of the pattern: **involvement**. This is not just the influencer's involvement, but that of others as well. Through their courage, their action, and their passion, they can move others to be involved and to join with them. When that happens, they have already become leaders! Why? Because they have influenced others to follow them into action to meet whatever challenge or need they are facing.

Finally, involvement leads to **change**. In many cases, the problem that troubled the influencer is resolved or fixed because of the person's initiative. The influencer protects the people, the honour of the nation, and his or her own integrity.

As we look at the examples of influencers in the Bible, we will see several different types of triggers that moved them to act, to involve others, and eventually to change the situation. It was not always a quick or easy process, but young leaders in the Bible followed this pattern to influence their peers and leaders to bring about change and save their people. Let's look at some examples of this pattern in action.

## DAVID

Israel was battling a mighty enemy. The Philistines had superior bronze weapons. One of the soldiers was a terrifyingly strong and tall champion, Goliath. He intimidated the Israelite soldiers, taunting them each day.

David, the youngest son in his family, had been left at home to watch the sheep while his older brothers fought in the war. He came to the battlefield to deliver food to them. But he saw the giant blaspheming God and mocking the armies of Israel. David asked some probing questions: "What will be done for the man who kills this Philistine and removes this disgrace from Israel? Who is this uncircumcised Philistine that he should defy the armies of the living God?" (1 Samuel 17:26).

David's first question, "What will be done for the man . . . ?" eventually alerted the leadership that David was available for the task and wanted to be involved. His second question focused upon the real issues. God's name was being defied. God's people were being mocked. David was motivated by a **cause**: the disgrace that was upon the nation of Israel, the chosen people of God. Therefore action needed to be taken to address those issues.

> Influencers can move others to be involved and to join with them. When that happens, they have already become leaders!

David was persistent with his questions and this angered his older brother. He told David off for being wicked, thinking David just wanted to abandon his shepherd duties to watch the exciting battle. But that rebuke didn't stop David. He brought up the same matter again with some other men (1 Samuel 17:30). Finally, the news reached the king of Israel that someone was concerned that God was being blasphemed and Israel was being mocked. King Saul sent for him.

Sometimes the way to have influence is to ask questions until the leadership hears someone wants to be involved and can help them move forward. If the questions we are asking, the actions we are proposing, or the changes we want to bring about can be shown to be in line with the goals and objectives of the leadership, they will be much more open to our proposals and desired outcomes.

To influence those in leadership positions, we need to understand their problems and concerns. Saul needed a champion to fight the enemy and deliver the nation. David was willing to fulfil that need and that gave him the opportunity to lead the battle.

We also need to convince our leaders that we can solve the problem. Saul needed to be persuaded by David that he should be allowed to fight the giant. Even though David's offer to battle Goliath would fulfil Saul's need for a champion, he was not convinced that David was the right person. Saul said, "You are not able to go out against this Philistine and fight him; you are only a young man, and he has been a warrior from his youth" (1 Samuel 17:33).

Speech coach David Greenberg says you prove that you have a solution to someone's pain by using "testimonials, data, and your own hard-won knowledge or experience".[36] David replied by telling Saul how he had killed both a lion and a bear and then said, "The Lord who rescued me from the paw of the lion and the paw of the bear will rescue me from the hand of this Philistine" (1 Samuel 17:37). With these words, David brought the discussion back to that which was distressing Saul. David offered Saul relief from what was bothering him, and so Saul agreed to David's request.

David asked questions and gave evidence of his ability to address the painful issue at hand. He influenced his leader to allow him to take **action** and fight Goliath. Once Goliath was killed, others became **involved**. The army that had been hiding in their tents went out and defeated the Philistines. This resulted in a **change** as the people of God were delivered.

David's Pattern of Proactive Influence

It is not enough to have a solution for an existing problem. We must also know how to let those in leadership know that we have the solution. Many leaders, like Saul, may be sceptical of your inexperience, but don't condemn them for their concerns. See this as an opportunity for you to provide evidence.

## Ask Questions

Let's explore how we can use David's technique of asking questions to become influencers. John Maxwell says that you only get answers to the questions you ask. For him, questions unlock and open doors, connect with people, cultivate humility, engage others in conversation, build better ideas, give us a different perspective, challenge your mindset, and get you out of ruts.[37] Every influencer can benefit from these outcomes of questions to make a difference.

When we ask questions, we must be ready and willing to

listen to the answers we receive, especially when we are asking questions of our leaders about things we feel need to be changed or improved. We need to hear their perspective, what they are thinking about the issue, and their concerns. This careful listening may give us clues as to the way forward and help us to understand how we might be able to influence the needed change. Maxwell and Dornan write:

> When you consistently listen to others, you never suffer for ideas. People love to contribute . . . If you give people opportunities to share their thoughts, and you listen with an open mind, there will always be a flow of new ideas. And even if you hear ideas that won't work, just listening to them can often spark other creative thoughts in you and others. You'll never know how close you are to a million-dollar idea unless you're willing to listen.[38]

If we ask questions of our leaders but already have our minds made up as to what the solution is, we could easily miss the opportunity to address the issue in a way that will enlist them as participants in our cause.

When we ask questions, we have to be sensitive and careful in the way and the attitude with which they are asked. We can ask questions for information and to bring issues to light. However, our attitude must always be respectful. We must never ask in an accusatory or a condescending manner. To do so will only raise walls between us and our leaders and will make them become defensive. When that happens, our ability to be an influencer will be seriously harmed or lost completely.

### Questions to Ask

Over the years I (Phil) have used two questions to influence situations:

"What was done well?"

"What could be done better the next time?"[39]

These two simple questions catalyze change. They start with analyzing the past and set goals for the future. They show where you have come from and explore where you are going. You can use these questions to evaluate any activity.

I began using these questions in a class I was teaching on preaching. We did in-class peer evaluations of the sermons that were preached. At first this was a bit intimidating for the students and they were reluctant to publicly criticize a fellow student. However, because the questions were positive in tone, and because I modelled the exercise, the class became quite adept at their use. The quality of their sermons immediately improved.

As students worked through the first question, "What did the preacher do well?" they saw the things that they should do or include when it was their turn to preach. These were the right answers from the past.

When they answered the second question, "What could the preacher do the next time to make this good sermon even better?" they saw what they should avoid or not do in their next sermon. This was the right question about the future.

Since that time, I have applied these questions in my life and my ministry as I have evaluated different situations and experiences I have gone through. There are times when my colleagues or my children will bring them up in our discussions and conversations regarding a wide variety of contexts.

> We must never ask in an accusatory or a condescending manner.

You might want to consider beginning a discipline of asking yourself what you have done and what you could do to improve. Keep a journal and at the end of the day ask yourself whether you did what you had planned to do that day, what you did well, and how you can improve. Record the answers. The advantage of writing these down is that you can occasionally review your progress – perhaps every month or every quarter. Then you can ask yourself larger questions to help you in setting goals and achieving them as an influencer:

- Where do I want to be? What goal do I want to achieve?
- Where am I now? What resources do I have?
- What obstacles are stopping me from getting to my destination?
- How do I get to my destination? What steps or strategies can I take?

These questions will be very helpful in your journey as a growing leader, enabling you to evaluate your progress towards your goals. Perhaps you have questions about the future. What are we going to do as a church to reach our generation? What are we going to do to help our nations in the areas of food security, education, unemployment, tribalism, addiction to alcohol and drugs, violence against women, trafficking and sexual abuse of children, and corruption? We could make an argument that the answers of the past have not worked, but the only way to know why they haven't worked is to evaluate them using questions such as "What worked well?" and "How can we improve?" As we ask the right questions about the past, we may find the answers we need to influence our generation.

## DANIEL

Four teenagers' lives had been completely uprooted. They used to belong to wealthy and respected families in their homeland. But their country had been defeated by a superpower nation. They had been taken as prisoners of war. As intelligent young men, they were being trained to serve the king of the foreign government that had invaded their country. The king wanted to erase their loyalty to their homeland and their religion. He was training them in the culture and dark magic of his country. The Bible tells us the story of these teenagers, Daniel and his friends under King Nebuchadnezzar.

As part of their training, the young men were offered the finest food in the land – the food that came from the king's own table. It was delicious meat and wine. However, eating it would mean betraying their Jewish identity and their religion. The food may have been unclean, offered to idols, or eating from the king's table may have obligated them to be loyal to the king no matter what. Daniel and his friends were foreign captives. They knew the king was ruthless and they could be killed for refusing to eat what the king provided.

Despite the danger, Daniel purposed in his heart to take a stand and not to eat that food: "But Daniel resolved not to defile himself with the royal food and wine, and he asked the chief official for permission not to defile himself this way" (Daniel 1:8).

The chief official could also get in trouble for disobeying the king's orders, so as part of his appeal Daniel proposed that they be given a strict vegetarian diet as a trial. This seemed reasonable to the chief official. A trial is a good way to influence people. Michael Zigarelli, commenting on this trial says:

> [Daniel] discerned that the only way the guard [the chief official] would grant his unorthodox – even dangerous – request would be if the guard saw for himself the wisdom of that request. The guard had to experience the result, not just hear about it. There needed to be some physical, tangible evidence for the guard to be persuaded. So, Daniel arranges for that evidence with his ten-day trial. Nothing short of brilliant.[40]

Why is Daniel's strategy brilliant? There are two reasons. First, whenever we propose to do something new or different, or what may seem risky, the trial period is a situation where the leader cannot lose. We put a time limit on it and if it works, the leader looks good. If it doesn't work, we can go back to the old way and nothing is lost.

Secondly, it was brilliant because Daniel appealed for a trial that included experiential evidence. Some leaders are sceptical at best and cynical at worst when receiving ideas from those who may not be in the official leadership loop. A pastor may not feel he can receive suggestions from a youth or an untrained layperson. However, if he can be shown through evidence the value and viability of the proposal, it may influence him to listen and give his support.

Serge Moscovici says: "Whenever a group, subgroup, or

individual is certain about something, influence cannot be used to bring about changes in their opinion or judgements."[41] But in contrast he says, "The more uncertain a person is in his opinions and judgements, the greater his propensity to be influenced."[42] What this means is that influencers need to introduce uncertainty regarding the situation into the mind and experience of the leader or group in which they are trying to bring change. A trial that produces evidence to the contrary of the settled certainty can move the leader from being closed to influence to being receptive of it.

**A trial is a good way to influence people.**

It is often effective to combine David's practice of asking questions with trial periods like Daniel and his friends suggested. For instance, an evangelistic group met regularly to pray for the land and held annual open-air preaching, but they were making little progress. Finally one member asked the leaders the right question: How were the converts from the outreaches followed up? How effectively was the current approach transforming their community?

The group realized that the open-air outreaches were not accomplishing their goals. Then, a member suggested that they try an approach they had never thought of before: reaching young people through a gathering of like-minded youth, then evaluating the outcome.

Over 100 youth attended the first conference. The quality of sessions and issues that were discussed gladdened the hearts of the leaders. In fact, one of the leaders saw it as not just a programme for the youth but also a capacity building event for them as leaders. Today, this has become an annual gathering. The initially sceptical leaders are driving the vision for the event and are involved in funding it.

Daniel's Pattern of Proactive Influence

We learn from Daniel and his friends that when we see something is wrong, or a decision being made that we don't believe is right, we can go to our authorities and ask them to reconsider their decision. We must have good reasons for making an appeal. An appeal is not for things that we don't like but for things that are really a moral issue or an outright mistake. Using an appeal for frivolous or non-essential matters dilutes the process and our efforts will be dismissed out of hand. The appeal process is for serious matters of practical importance and where a biblical principle is being ignored or violated.

Daniel's appeal included a suggested **action**. Leaders don't appreciate it when people just come to them with problems. They say, "If you bring me a problem, come with a solution." If you don't bring a possible approach to resolve the issue, you will come across as a whiner and complainer instead of an influencer. Daniel is a good example of this statement by Lois Wyse, the advertising executive: "The only people in the world who can change things are those who can sell ideas."[43]

Daniel, through his appeal and evidenced-based trial, was able to sell his idea for an adjustment in the captives' diet. Daniel's action led to the **involvement** of the leader in the trial, and eventually brought a **change** in the diet of all four of the Hebrew young men who were in the king's training programme as we see in verse 16: "So the guard took away their choice food and the wine to drink and gave them vegetables instead."

When you go to your leader wanting to change something, suggest an alternative. If you cannot change the whole system, suggest it at least for yourself. Show them how this will not hinder their goals. If God so leads you, you might offer a trial period like Daniel and his friends did.

### Set an Example

Because Daniel and his friends maintained their integrity, later in the book of Daniel they were able to resist the king's pressure to worship idols and to speak to the king on God's behalf. When we maintain our integrity, we are being influenced by God, who can then use us more powerfully to influence others.

This is a great way for us to lead when we do not have a position of leadership. Perhaps you see something in your workplace, church, or family that you cannot participate in without sacrificing your own integrity. Perhaps you cannot change the whole system. However, you can find a way not to participate in the morally compromising behaviour. Keshavan Nair, writes: "Those of us not in power have a responsibility to raise our standards so our leaders will have to follow."[44]

Living by a higher standard can have an influence. In a test hall during his first semester on campus, a student was troubled to find that the majority of the students were copying from each other or the textbook. He approached two of his Christian friends in the class. They laughed at him for being too strict. A Christian student leader even told him that the Scriptures said we should help especially those who are of the household of faith! The new student was from a different culture, trying to fit in and make friends during his first semester. But he resolved to hold on to his convictions. Throughout his time on campus, he spoke to his classmates about the danger of cheating in examinations. Some called him names, but others stood with him. Eventually, he graduated as the best student in the department, without cheating. One of the lecturers in the department heard about his reputation and even gave him one of his textbooks as an encouragement!

Raising our standards of life and behaviour to a high level is a wonderful way to influence our leaders and our peers. In a non-confrontational way (though it may be threatening and convicting) we can lead others to change their ways of thinking and behaving by quietly living out our faith. This is very much in line with the challenge that Paul gives Timothy in 1 Timothy 4:12: "Don't let anyone look down on you because you are young, but set an example for the believers [including those who are older than you and are in positions of authority] in speech, in conduct, in love, in faith and in purity."

When I (Phil) was a pastor of a church in the US, I had a young man who strongly opposed abortion. His activity in the pro-life movement eventually led many in our church, including me, to join some of the events that were organized in our town to peacefully stand against the killing of babies. We opposed abortion as a congregation, but his influence helped us to move out in a more public and active way against this great evil. One person's conviction and example can eventually influence others to act as well.

## Be Patient

Both David and Daniel saw a problem. David saw that his nation was being shamed and his God was being mocked. He took action to restore his nation's honour. Daniel's and his friends' integrity was at stake. He took the initiative to preserve his individual integrity. Whether the problem you see affects your whole nation or only the personal morality of you and a few friends, you can be a proactive influencer by speaking out. Perhaps God has shown you this problem because you are the one he is calling to change the situation.

There were many petty traders and local entrepreneurs in Ezekiel Kyauta's community. He and his team asked, "How can we enhance their lives and businesses?" They started up a cooperative with leaders. A few of them learned more at a workshop organized by a forum where Ezekiel serves as secretary. After one year they were fully registered, with members getting a dividend from their monthly contributions. He took the initiative by asking questions, and the cooperative has helped local businesses expand.

Like Daniel, David, Godiya, or Ezekiel, you can take the initiative and proactively begin to influence your community. However, be aware that these steps and the use of the various triggers do not constitute a magical formula that will work every time. The leadership that we are trying to influence may not respond in the way we desire or in any way at all. But even if they do not respond, God

We must faithfully do what we can do and trust God to do what only he can do.

calls us to be faithful and to have endurance and to persevere. God is the ultimate change agent in control of all things and people, and he is working out his plan for the ages. Therefore, we must faithfully do what we can do and trust God to do what only he can do according to his sovereign will and time. Never limit what God can do through you when you take that first step.

## QUESTIONS FOR DISCUSSION AND PERSONAL APPLICATION

1. Is there a situation in your life or ministry that you feel needs to be changed? Would asking questions, an appeal, a trial, or setting an example enable you to begin to address the issue?

2. As you begin to pray and think about this trigger, what action or actions do you believe God would have you take to begin to influence others to bring about the desired change?

3. As you begin to plan for taking action, are there others that you can encourage to become involved with you as you seek to bring about change?

4. If you follow through with the process and change doesn't happen immediately, what will be your plan of action? It is at this point that you might want to wait for a period of time and then appeal to the authority again.

_______________________________________________

_______________________________________________

_______________________________________________

_______________________________________________

_______________________________________________

_______________________________________________

_______________________________________________

CHAPTER FIVE

# AN INFLUENCER'S HEART

Perhaps the most important quality that the African leadership needs to embrace . . . is a sense of service to their people.[45]

— WANGARI MAATHAI —

Peter Galadima is an itinerant minister committed to reaching Muslims and locals. While serving in the field, he eats after everyone else has been served and often fasts for days before an outreach. His prayers show his burden for souls. If something affects a team member, he takes it upon himself to resolve the matter. He buys books and gives them to young members of his outreach team. If you spend time with him, you will recognize the heart of an influencer.

You have learned how to influence others. But what should you influence them towards? Influence can be used to help or hurt others, to bring positive or negative change. Now that you have the power of knowing how to influence, it is very important that you exercise it with responsibility. In this chapter, we encourage you to form the heart attitude of a godly influencer like Peter Galadima who God can use to accomplish his plan.

## SELFISH FORCE

One Bible story shows us the contrast between two groups who used their influence for positive and negative change. After King Solomon died, his son Rehoboam became king of Israel (1 Kings 12). The people came to Rehoboam and asked for relief from the harsh labour and the heavy yoke they had experienced under the rule of Solomon. If he granted their request, they were ready to submit to Rehoboam's rule and to serve him. Rehoboam sought advice from two groups of influencers: the elders who had served in Solomon's court and the young men who were his peers.

The elders said, "If today you will be a servant to these people and serve them and give them a favorable answer, they will always be your servants" (1 Kings 12:7). They wanted what was best for Rehoboam. They wanted him to have loyal subjects. They also wanted what was best for the people. They had compassion on the overworked labourers. So they gave selfless and humble advice based on their experience.

The Elders' Pattern of Proactive Influence

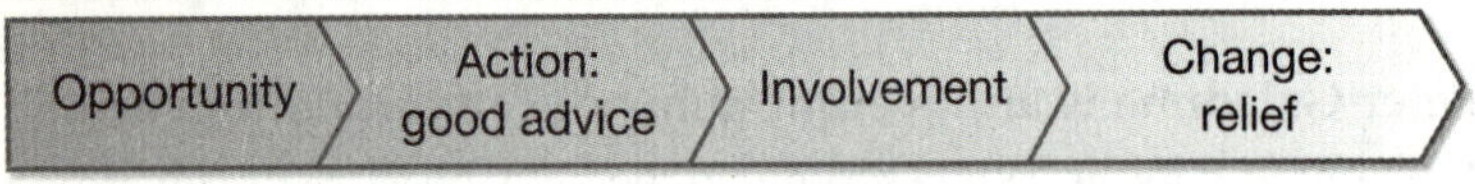


The young men told Rehoboam he should be harsher and more domineering than his father. They did not have the interests of the people in mind. They counselled him to oppress the people when the people had asked for mercy and relief. They didn't have Rehoboam's interests in mind, or at least they were unaware of how this would damage his authority. They wanted Rehoboam to use force, not influence, to control the people. It seems their hearts were greedy for power. The young men had grown up with Rehoboam and were now serving him (1 Kings 12:8). They were now in the place of influence, power, and decision-making. Now they could make their mark. I can imagine that they might have felt the exhilaration of exercising power. Maybe they felt that the elders under Solomon were too old-fashioned, and said to themselves, "The elders' time for influencing the leader and affairs of state is over. Now is the time for the younger generation to step up and shape policy!"

Rehoboam gave in to the influence of his peers. The people had asked for positive change but instead they received a promise of a harsher version of their present state. The northern tribes revolted against Rehoboam. The nation was divided and never reunited again.

The Young Men's Pattern of Proactive Influence

The young men were successful in influencing Rehoboam, but their hearts were selfish. The change they caused backfired because they did not care about others. They thought force was the way to gain followers instead of servant leadership. Instead of becoming powerful and famous, these young men's legacy was a terrible tragedy – Rehoboam lost many followers.

We learn an important lesson from these young men. When we are close to a leader and have the opportunity to influence, it can be tempting to push our own selfish interests. We can seek power more than we want to serve people. We are tired of being told what to do by our seniors, so as soon as we have the opportunity to use force, we bully others.

**The heart of influence is not force, but service.**

But this is not a godly way or even an effective way to cause change. The heart of influence is not force, but service. It is about being influenced by God to influence others to become all he has for them to be. When we put away our pride and desire for power, we can be effective influencers and create positive change for the whole society. If we focus on our selfish goals, we will lose the opportunity to create change, and even the power and followers we have will start to slip away from us.

Tusfe led the young student Sali to the Lord. She respected him as a spiritual mentor and someone she could trust. Unfortunately, Tusfe got Sali pregnant. When his leaders confronted him, he denied responsibility until the facts forced him to confess that he was responsible. His actions had far-reaching consequences. They affected the faith of Sali and other fellowship members and painted a wrong picture to non-Christians. Tusfe had an opportunity to influence someone towards godliness. But he abused his influence for his own immoral and selfish desires. You should intentionally watch against using your influence for selfish or sinful ends!

In complete contrast to Tusfe, a young man shared with his colleagues that he and his wife were finding it tough to commute daily to the office with a newborn baby. He asked them to pray for a car for his family. A few days later, his mentor called the young father to his house and presented him with the key of his only family car! The mentor was moved to generosity even though his own family would need to go back to using public transport. What selflessness!

## SERVANT COMPASSION

In contrast to Rehoboam's advisors, other Bible characters were good examples of servant compassion. One young girl was captured by a marauding band from Aram. She became a slave to the wife of Naaman, the Aramean army commander (2 Kings 5). Unfortunately, Naaman had leprosy.

His wife's young slave knew a prophet who could heal him. The girl could have been bitter and revengeful. She could have decided not to help him, thinking he deserved the leprosy. But instead, she cared about her master. In compassion, she said, "If only my master would see the prophet who is in Samaria! He would cure him of his leprosy" (2 Kings 5:3).

Naaman was touched by her concern. He accepted her influence and went to see the prophet Elisha. In the end, God used Elisha to heal Naaman. As a result, Naaman became a worshipper of the one true God! This influencer's compassionate heart glorified God. We still read about her thousands of years later. When you think compassionately of others, God can use you to bring him glory and make an eternal mark in the sands of time.

Choosing to love someone who has wronged you is a difficult task but not an impossible one. I (Hankuri) was persecuted by Muslims during my campus days. This led to my being expelled from the university in my final year and kept me away from my state capital for 10 years. Yet I discovered that I had a growing love for Muslim students on campus. I encouraged Christian students to demonstrate the love of Christ by spending time in prayer for their Muslim friends and then presenting them with a gift. These students and I have learned that we can even influence people when the world may think we should be bitter towards them.

Another compassionate servant was Ebed-Melech, an official in the royal palace in Judah who originally came from the African nation of Cush. He noticed that the officials of Jerusalem were upset with the prophet Jeremiah warning God's people to repent. They had Jeremiah taken prisoner and thrown into a cistern where he sank down in the mud.

Ebed-Melech knew this was wrong. He decided to stand against these powerful and wicked officials, a dangerous decision, since the king had supported their action and Ebed-Melech was only a foreigner. He could have thought it wasn't his concern. If these men were ready to kill Jeremiah, they probably could imprison him, the interfering foreigner.

But Ebed-Melech chose to do what was right. He had compassion on Jeremiah and stood up against the injustice. He went to King Zedekiah and told him that Jeremiah would starve to death in the cistern. He requested permission to rescue Jeremiah. His actions and words influenced his boss, the king, to intervene in Jeremiah's case and to save the prophet's life.

Just like in the time of the servant girl and Ebed-Melech, our world has all kinds of suffering and pain. In our communities we have people imprisoned without being convicted, schools abandoned in rural communities without infrastructure, relatives living in camps for internally displaced persons and refugees, women abused by their husbands, young girls forced into early marriages, students targeted by lecturers for refusing to yield to their demand for sex or money.

When we see physical, emotional, and spiritual anguish, God may be calling us to an opportunity for influence. Paul says, "Carry each other's burdens, and in this way you will fulfill the law of Christ" (Galatians 6:2). We can bear a portion of someone else's suffering by listening to them and helping them to go through their trial. We may even be able to help them come out of that painful situation by connecting them to someone else, advocating for them, or generously providing for their needs. God has given us compassion to be influencers in his image.

After an attack by Fulani herdsmen not far from where I (Hankuri) live in Nigeria, over 30,000 families were displaced. Many had lost their loved ones and property worth millions in cash. Some of the students I worked with had parents and siblings in the camps. We prayed for them in our fellowship, but we were moved to do more. We felt that every soul matters to God, so if we could help just one person for the glory of God, then we would have demonstrated the love of Christ. We began using social media and phone calls to share stories and pictures of the displaced people. We asked for resources from students and partners. People responded! We were able to provide foodstuffs, clothes, and trauma counselling to the displaced families. We cut the men's hair and plaited the women's hair. We taught them skills, found scholarships for some of their children, and gave seed capital to a few women to help them start over again. We were even able to advocate for them to be relocated back home and have some of their property replaced. We did not have the money at the time we started this initiative. But God gave us the ability to influence people for his cause.

Look around you. What can you do even without a position of leadership?

## WORLDLY VALUES VERSUS GOD-FEARING VALUES

An influencer's heart should also fear God rather than worshipping worldly values.

Joash became king of Judah. He was a godly king because he had a godly influencer – Jehoiada the priest. The wicked Queen Athaliah had usurped power and killed all the rightful heirs to the throne (2 Kings 11), but a godly woman had kept Joash safe.

When he was seven years old, Jehoiada took Joash out of hiding and put him on the throne. He protected and taught Joash how to rule. So "Joash did what was right in the eyes of the Lord all the years Jehoiada the priest instructed him" (2 Kings 12:2). Joash influenced the nation in the worship of the Lord. He decided to restore the temple of the Lord. The Levites delayed in making the necessary repairs, but Joash persisted and rebuked them for their inaction (2 Kings 12:7). Up until this point, Joash would have been numbered among the good kings of Judah.

But when Jehoiada died, King Joash came under the negative influence of ungodly advisers and completely reversed his direction! "After the death of Jehoiada, the officials of Judah came and paid homage to the king, and he listened to them. They abandoned the temple of the Lord, the God of their ancestors, and worshiped Asherah poles and idols" (2 Chronicles 24:17-18).

This is bad enough as it is, but Joash's decline went even further. There was opportunity to receive further positive influence. Instead, Joash led the people to continue to rebel, rejecting what they had known to be true and persisting in their new path of evil: "Although the Lord sent prophets to the people to bring them back to him, and although they testified against them, they would not listen" (2 Chronicles 24:19).

Finally, God sent Jehoiada's son, a prophet named Zechariah, to warn them that they would not prosper. They had abandoned the Lord, so the Lord would abandon them (2 Chronicles 24:20). One would have thought that surely when Joash saw Zechariah, he would have remembered Jehoiada. He would have thought fondly of the godly man who had raised him and had taught him everything he knew. He would have remembered that without Jehoiada, he would never have become king and would probably have been killed long ago. He would have realized how far he had strayed and repent. But "King Joash did not remember the kindness Zechariah's father Jehoiada had shown him but killed his son" (2 Chronicles 24:22). What a tragedy!

Joash was a godly influencer who became a wicked and worldly influencer. Why did Joash change? I wonder if it could be inferred from the fact that the officials, the influencers, "came and paid homage" to him. Perhaps that homage flattered him and appealed to his pride.

**We must follow God rather than being tempted by flattery. We must love God and people rather than our own interests.**

To be influencers for positive change, we must follow God rather than being tempted by the flattery and false idols of this world. To be compassionate servants rather than using selfish force, we must protect our hearts. We must love God and people rather than our own interests.

## WHO INFLUENCES THE INFLUENCER?

As we see in the story of Joash, even as influencers we are influenced by others. Joash was influenced for good by Jehoiada, but for evil by his officials. His story warns us of how powerfully others can influence us.

The book of Proverbs gives us strong warnings as well. Not everyone leads us in the right path:

> My son, if sinful men entice you,
> do not give in to them.
> If they say, "Come along with us [to do all sorts of evil and wickedness] . . ."
> my son, do not go along with them,
> do not set foot on their paths (Proverbs 1:10-11, 15).

Those who follow these negative influencers eventually lose their lives. People who try to become rich quickly through violence think they are plotting the destruction of others, but really they are setting a trap for their own destruction. They "lie in wait for their own blood" (Proverbs 1:18).

We need to discern the intentions of the people around us:

> Enemies disguise themselves with their lips,
> but in their hearts they harbor deceit.
> Though their speech is charming, do not believe them,
> for seven abominations fill their hearts (Proverbs 26:24-25).

We also need to be careful of those we choose to give us counsel and advice:

> Walk with the wise and become wise,
> for a companion of fools suffers harm (Proverbs 13:20).

All these proverbs make it clear that the way to avoid being affected by negative influence is to choose one's relationships carefully and wisely. Positive and godly companions will lead us in the path of righteousness and help to keep us there.

In the Scriptures we have examples of people like David who was influenced by Jonathan; Esther who was influenced by Mordecai; Joshua who was influenced by Moses; the disciples who were influenced by Jesus Christ; and Timothy who was influenced by his mother, his grandmother, and Paul. The books you read and the friends you keep also influence you. Whatever you feed your mind with will certainly shape your life and your influence. To form the godly heart of an influencer, we need to surround ourselves with godly influencers.

## QUESTIONS FOR DISCUSSION AND PERSONAL APPLICATION

1. Examine who your advisors are as you seek to be an influencer and bring about change. Simply put, "As an influencer, who is influencing you?" Are your advisors godly people who will give wise and scriptural advice?

2. What can we do to protect ourselves from negative influencers?

3. What are some injustices in your community? Who do you feel compassion toward? What small action could you take to begin to influence that situation?

CHAPTER SIX

# WHEN CHALLENGES COME

Resistance can come in many forms . . . When, where, and how challenges will surface is somewhat unpredictable . . . The church in change cannot and should not always avoid conflict. It needs wisdom when confrontation arises.[46]

— JIM HERRINGTON, MIKE BONEM, AND JAMES H. FURR —

Joseph Mafolase encountered Christ on campus and wanted to share the gospel with young people in his church, which was an African Independent Church. He decided to start teaching Sunday school classes and being more involved in the youth arm of his church. He taught on the basics of salvation and how it results in a changed lifestyle. Some of the youth trusted Jesus Christ. They started breaking away from bad relationships, obeying their parents, embracing the gospel, and sharing it with others. Instead of celebrating, the elders in the church stopped him from holding weekly prayers and teaching the youth. They reprimanded Joseph for doing what young people were not expected to do.

## THE EFFECTIVE INFLUENCER CAUSES CONFLICT

It may come as a surprise, but when a person starts to influence, conflict will result. When we say an influencer causes conflict, we don't mean that you should be aggressive or harsh. You may have the best of motives and the deepest love and concern for the organization or group you want to influence. You may want to challenge traditions and outdated modes of operation to improve things and have no intention of offending anyone.

Still, simply by proposing a new direction and change, you are challenging the status quo. People like the way things are. People are comfortable with the familiar, with what they have always known. Changes will disrupt routine and move people out and away from their comfort zone. As an influencer, you should expect resistance and disagreement.

The key is not simply to cause conflict, but also to resolve the conflict.[47] Hopefully the conflict will be resolved in the direction of the change you desire. If the conflict is resolved by maintaining things as they have always been, there has been no influence.

Change is a process and it takes time. You may be proposing a change or action that is a minority viewpoint. Persuading people will be a difficult struggle. You will need to cause people to question what they have known, cast a vision for what could be, and execute a plan. This takes commitment and perseverance. Serge Moscovici comments that any minority that brings about genuine innovation must start and continue for a certain length of time, with no advantages in the way of power, status, resources, or competence.[48] You will need to be patient and persistent in your efforts. You have to constantly push little by little. However, if you get impatient and push too hard, you may rush things and cause more conflict than necessary.[49]

In this chapter, we will talk about the conflict people in the Bible experienced when they tried to influence. We will learn from them how they resolved the conflict and succeeded in their influence.

## REMEMBER YOUR CALLING

As a young pastor, I (Phil) was serving in a small church. No matter what I tried to do to move the congregation in a new direction, we seemed to fail or were met with little enthusiasm. It was discouraging as we were struggling to grow and make an impact on our community. I remember telling my wife one Sunday evening, "I feel like just getting a job driving a lorry. But I can't because I know that God has called me to be a pastor."

Stories like Amos's story in the Bible are great sources of

encouragement to remaining faithful to our calling. Amos was a prophet in the Bible who spoke messages from God. He was fearlessly committed to telling the truth about the evils of his society. Amos proclaimed that God would judge Israel for oppressing the poor and ignoring God's word.

Amos also spoke out against the idolatry in Israel. King Jeroboam had set up centres for false worship because he had broken away from Judah, where God's real temple was. The king didn't want his people travelling to worship in the temple in Jerusalem under another king's control (1 Kings 12:25-32). He made an altar in Bethel, a city in southern Israel, where Israelites could worship a golden calf with false priests. Amos proclaimed:

> "On the day I punish Israel for her sins,
> I will destroy the altars of Bethel;
> the horns of the altar will be cut off
> and fall to the ground.
> I will tear down the winter house
> along with the summer house;
> the houses adorned with ivory will be destroyed
> and the mansions will be demolished,"
> declares the Lord (Amos 3:14-15).

As you can imagine, Amos's influence caused conflict. People didn't want to hear God would judge them for their sins! One day, a false priest from Bethel called Amaziah confronted Amos. He told him to go back to the land of Judah if he must prophesy, but "Don't prophesy anymore at Bethel, because this is the king's sanctuary and the temple of the kingdom" (Amos 7:13). Amaziah mentioned the king as a threat to Amos, using the power and position of the king to intimidate Amos. He used the spiritual authority of the temple of Bethel to try to scare Amos and put him in his place.

But Amos was not intimidated. He replied that God had called him specifically to prophesy to Israel: "I was neither a prophet nor the son of a prophet, but I was a shepherd and I also took care of sycamore-fig trees. But the Lord took me from tending the flock and said to me, 'Go, prophesy to my people Israel'" (Amos 7:14-15).

It was true that Amos had no position – he had not been a professional prophet before. His father was not a prophet, so he had no training for that office. He was just an ordinary person. In fact, he was a "nobody" in the eyes of Jewish society; shepherds and farmers were on the low end of the social scale.

Most of us can identify with Amos. When someone comes to tell us we have no right to speak out for change, we cannot respond by listing our formal qualifications or positions. We are just ordinary people who are concerned to make a change for God.

**Amos had the courage to be an influencer because God had a call on his life that could not be ignored.**

But the rest of Amos's response is important. He says that God called him to prophesy to Israel. The spiritual authority of the temple at Bethel did not matter compared to God's instruction. The king's power was nothing compared to God's power. Amaziah wanted him to leave Israel. Amos knew God wanted him there. Amos could not accept what Amaziah told him to do because God had already told him what he must do.

Amos had the courage to be an influencer because God had a call on his life that could not be ignored. How can we be confident that we have been called by God? In general terms, the divine call of God in our lives is not something mysterious. It is the call to obedience. It is the call to service. It is the call to surrender our life and our will to live out the implications of the gospel as children of God. Dallas Willard writes:

> The call of Christ today is the same as it was when he left us here to serve him "even to the end of the age" (Matthew 28:20). We have not yet come to the "end of the age". That call is to be his apprentices, alive in the power of God, learning to do all he

> said to do, leading others into apprenticeship to him, and also teaching them how to do everything he said.[50]

However, in specific terms, it is sometimes harder to identify what the divine call is. It does not have to be a blinding light with Jesus himself appearing and speaking to us like Paul experienced on the Damascus road. Usually it is a quiet and growing awareness in one's inner being that God is asking us to be involved in a certain ministry or with a certain group or individual. As we respond to God's general call to follow and obey him, he will lead us into specific areas of service and influence.

When we look at church history, we see that God has used many who did not hold an official position. They simply courageously followed through on God's calling because they were committed to be used of God to be influencers for change. One such example is Martin Luther, who as a monk challenged the hierarchy of the Roman Catholic Church in the area of selling indulgences. An indulgence was a piece of paper that guaranteed the release of a person's soul from purgatory. The pope was using the sale of these indulgences to finance his building projects. Luther rightly pointed out that this was unbiblical. When he first published his objections in what is known as *The Ninety-Five Theses,* he did not know the great changes that his actions would bring about. This was the beginning of the Protestant Reformation.

God can use circumstances to call us into action. For example, God may bring an unexpected opportunity into our life. As we respond to it, we may find that we are being drawn to do something. We can examine ourselves by asking questions like these:

- Is my concern in line with God's heart? For instance, am I standing up for God's truth or advocating for others with his compassion?
- Am I using godly methods?
- Is there a skill, burden, relationship, resource, or other way God has given me to influence the situation?

We should also pray and seek counsel from godly counsellors who can give us wise insight. Their feedback can help to confirm that God is truly guiding us to become involved. They can encourage us when we face hardships while trying to change the situation.

When people challenge or threaten us as influencers, we need to remember why we are advocating for change. If God has called us, we do not need to be afraid. We can be encouraged that he will use us for his purposes. When we face opposition, we can stand strong. We move forward with confidence. If God is for us, who can be against us (Romans 8:31)?

## CHOOSE WISELY

Sometimes we face conflict as influencers because we advocate for too many changes or choose an unimportant issue and devote our energy to it. This kind of conflict can often be avoided from the beginning.

Many years ago, someone gave me (Phil) some advice about being a parent. He said, "Choose your battles carefully." What he was saying is that when it comes to dealing with your children there are some things and issues that are just not worth fighting about.

The same is true of an influencer who is not in an official position of leadership. We may see a number of things that we would like changed. We may believe certain methods or procedures could be done differently. However, if we decide to fight every issue and oppose every decision, we will be labelled as negative. If this happens, we will lose trust and the opportunity to be an influencer for change. We only have so much energy, time, and resources. We shouldn't waste our efforts on minor issues or we will have nothing left for influencing change on more important matters.

Choose your battles carefully and wisely. Discern the degree of importance and urgency of the social issue or organizational change you want. Some things you may want to change may be based on personal preference and not on principle. If the concern is about material things like buildings or facilities, interpretation of facts, or personal taste, then these are not priorities for your focus. Ask yourself, "What value is at stake? Is there a spiritual or scriptural problem?" Identify the root issues and focus on influencing those. Will the resulting change be worth the cost to achieve it?

## COUNT THE COST AND COMMIT

Sometimes you may choose a very important cause that brings great conflict or even danger. In that case, you will need great courage to commit to influence.

Esther was a Jew living as an exile in the land of the foreign superpower, Persia. She became the wife of the king but kept her Jewish identity secret. Then her people were threatened with genocide. A noble close to the king hated her people. He got the king's permission to kill Jews throughout the kingdom: "Dispatches were sent by couriers to all the king's provinces with the order to destroy, kill and annihilate all the Jews – young and old, women and children – on a single day . . . " (Esther 3:13).

Esther had to take action. She and her people were going to be destroyed. Her cousin Mordecai told her to go into the throne room of her husband the king. She had not been invited. The law stated that going into the throne room without an invitation was punishable by death. If the king was feeling merciful, he might extend his sceptre to the offender and thereby save that person's life.

For Esther to influence the situation, she faced a conflict with the law. She would risk her life. Sometimes to be an influential leader we must be willing to take a risk. In the midst of a crisis, "risk is like change; it's not a choice."[51] However, we need to be wise about what risks we take.

Esther knew she only had one opportunity to start the influencing process. She needed to be sure that she had the courage and commitment to see the process through to the end. She was not foolish or rash, diving into conflict for a thrill. She realized how dangerous her decision was, but she also cared deeply about her people.

So Esther considered carefully what she should do. She listened to Mordecai's godly advice. Mordecai encouraged her that God had given her influence for this situation. He said, "For if you remain silent at this time, relief and deliverance for the Jews will arise from another place, but you and your father's family will perish. And who knows but that you have come to your royal position for such a time as this?" (Esther 4:14).

Esther also asked Mordecai to fast and pray with her and her servants. She asked for God's favour. Then Esther went to see the king. The king spared her life. She was able to expose the plot of Haman to annihilate the Jews. She appealed to the king to save her people. The king approved a plan that enabled the Jews to defend themselves and to take revenge upon their enemies.

Esther brought about a change in the law of the land and in the status of the Jews. A young woman took a great risk. Her courageous action influenced the course of history in that nation.

When we choose to influence a situation, the challenges we face may require us to take great personal risks. We need to weigh whether we are committed to the cause no matter what the cost. It is better not to start than to begin the process and give up when things get difficult or conflict arises. Quitting can damage trust and make it difficult to start again. Knowing that we will face conflict, we should ask God what he wants us to do and listen to godly advisors as Esther did. We can mobilize people to fast and pray with us. We can focus on our concern for others in a situation that affects them. Once we know what we need to do, we can act with courage despite the risks.

It is better not to start than to begin the process and give up.

In 2018, 106 schoolgirls were kidnapped by the Boko Haram terrorist group in Nigeria. Rev Gideon Para-Mallam began a strong advocacy campaign for their release. Five died in captivity, but a hundred were later released. However, Leah Sheribu, only fourteen when she was kidnapped, refused to convert to Islam so she has not been released. Although anyone who speaks against Boko Haram becomes a target, Rev Para-Mallam has continued to call on the federal government, Boko Haram, security forces, and other relevant agencies to ensure Leah is released. He has granted interviews to media houses, organized prayer meetings, produced a short documentary, organized advocacy events, provided shelter and guidance for Leah's parents, and spoken to both Muslim and Christian leaders to take action. Rev Para-Mallam is an example of courage to act despite the risk.

## LOVE YOUR DIFFICULT LEADER

Jonathan and his father King Saul had a difficult relationship. Remember the story about the warfare between the Philistines and Israel (1 Samuel 13–14)? Let's look a little closer at the surrounding events.

In the first battle between the two nations, Jonathan defeated the Philistines at Geba (1 Samuel 13:1-4). But it is Saul who blew the trumpet and took the credit for the victory. "So all Israel heard the news: 'Saul has attacked the Philistine outpost'" (1 Samuel 13:4). Did Saul attack the outpost? No.

After Jonathan climbed the hill with his armour bearer and initiated the second battle with the Philistines, Saul foolishly bound his army with an oath: "Cursed be anyone who eats food before evening comes, before I have avenged myself on my enemies!" (1 Samuel 14:24). At this point the battle was basically won because of what Jonathan did, but Saul tried to imply that he was the one pushing the action and tried to claim the credit.

Jonathan, who did not hear the curse, ate a small bit of honey. When the battle was over, Saul found that Jonathan had disobeyed his order. Instead of praising his son for bringing Israel victory, he was determined to kill Jonathan for disobeying without knowing it. What a terrible father-son relationship! Fortunately, the people would not allow Jonathan to die because they knew he was the one who had brought about their deliverance (1 Samuel 14:45).

Saul was truly a difficult leader. He was threatened by David's victories. After David killed Goliath, the women of Israel sang higher praise to David than to Saul: "Saul has slain his thousands, and David his tens of thousands" (1 Samuel 18:7). Saul's response was anger and jealousy against David: "Saul was very angry; this refrain displeased him greatly. 'They have credited David with tens of thousands,' he thought, 'but me with only thousands. What more can he get but the kingdom?' And from that time on Saul kept a close eye on David" (1 Samuel 18:8-9). Eventually Saul tried to kill both Jonathan and David by throwing his javelin at them. Is there a more difficult leader than this?

Sadly, many influencers face similar situations when they try to bring about change in their church or organization. As your influence grows, leaders might turn against you because they feel their own position is threatened. They may try to marginalize or eliminate you entirely from the organization and leadership.

How should we respond to this conflict? It can be very frustrating and discouraging for influencers when leaders resist the direction we are advocating. If we are not careful, we can become angry and bitter. A wrong attitude is not godly.

We see that while Jonathan advocated for change, especially in the way King Saul treated David, he continued to relate with his father, fighting alongside him, and submitting to his leadership whenever possible. Mordecai also continued to relate with Esther even when he didn't know if she would betray her people. Esther continued to relate with Haman until she executed her plan. Despite the opposition that the Pharisees mounted against Jesus, he did not walk away from them. He focused on what God had sent him to do in their midst, and some Pharisees ended up secretly following him.

We must resist the temptation to resent our leaders and walk the path of love instead. Martin Luther King Jr said, "Love is the only force capable of transforming an enemy into friend."[52] In fact, having a loving attitude and acting in love toward our leaders and the people we are trying to influence may be the biggest factor in bringing about the change we want to see.

How does this look in real life? Perhaps we can see by using the characteristics of love in 1 Corinthians 13:4-7 to describe how influencers should love:

> Influencers are patient, influencers are kind. They do not envy the success of others or boast about their own. They are not rude nor do they seek to get their own way. Influencers do not get angry or frustrated easily. They don't keep a record of the number of times they have been wronged or of those who have ill-treated them. Influencers do not delight in evil but rejoice with the truth. Influencers always protect, always trust, always hope for the best. Influencers never quit (my paraphrase).[53]

Loving leaders does not mean that you join them if they are doing wrong. It means, like Jonathan, you love Saul as your father but still speak for the cause you believe in or for the change you want to see. Being patient with your leaders in seeking to bring change also means you keep on doing what you are assigned to do well and wait for the next opportunity to propose change again. It means thinking of creative and innovative ways of sharing your view with the leader, studying how the leader thinks, and seeking the best way to approach him or her again. Sometimes your biggest opportunity for influence will be your ability to stay with the leader despite his or her rejection of your first recommendation. Always remember that if the change you want to bring is from the Lord, he can bring the opportunity at the right time.

## PRAY AND LISTEN TO GOD

Sometimes the conflict we face as influencers is not from outside, but from inside. We may be discouraged in the process for change and struggle to find motivation to do what we initially set out to do. We want to change others, but we find we first need to be transformed ourselves. One cannot lead others further than they themselves have travelled.

The prophet Habakkuk faced an internal conflict. He witnessed rampant wickedness, injustice, and violence in Judah. Yet it seemed like God was doing nothing. He prayed, but God seemed not to answer. He cried out, but God did not save. In fact, Habakkuk blamed God for tolerating wrong! He complained to God in prayer.

God responded by saying he would use the evil Babylonians to punish his people. This sounded even worse to Habakkuk. How could a holy God use them as instruments of judgement when the Babylonians were even more wicked than the Israelites?

Habakkuk's confusion and internal conflict was beginning the process of personal change. Without conflict, there is no influence. When our old ways of understanding no longer make sense, we must reflect critically on what we believed to be true. That is the moment we are most open for transformation.[54] Our self-reflection can lead to deeper understanding of what we believe or it can change our belief system to a clear and better understanding of the truth.

Habakkuk resolved this internal conflict by questioning God. When our experience and our understanding of God do not seem to match, we do not have to abandon our faith in God. Instead, Habakkuk took his doubts and questions to God. He patiently waited for God to help him through his disorientation. Faustin Ntamushobora comments:

> The prophet, finding himself sinking in the deepest hole and overwhelmed, raised himself up above the judgment and reason of men. He then came near to God so he might see from on high the events that took place on earth and not judge according to the understanding of his own flesh but by the light of the Holy Spirit![55]

This led to God's involvement in the life of Habakkuk. God responded and explained that the Babylonians, too ,would be punished for their pride. Just because God used them to punish Judah's sin did not mean that he approved of their sin. He had a sovereign plan.

God patiently dealt with his prophet. Habakkuk's understanding of God and his sovereign ways changed. He developed a stronger relationship with God and was able to trust and rest in him (Habakkuk 3). Ntamushobora summarizes this transformation:

> Habakkuk made a personal response to God by accepting God's will in his life despite the circumstances during the time of joy and sadness . . . Habakkuk had been profoundly challenged and *changed* by the answers he received from the Lord. He was a different man. Instead of complaining, he turned to praising (emphasis mine).[56]

He underwent a profound change in the way he looked at God and the world as he responded to the revelations he received from God.

Conflict will surely come when you try to influence. It is part of the process of bringing change. Even Jesus, greatest influencer of all time, faced conflict. He was a great teacher and miracle worker. But his greatest influence came from the challenges he faced. People who opposed him eventually crucified him, but that led to the salvation of the whole world. You cannot avoid challenges, but you can choose how to respond to them. When conflict arises, remember your calling and resolve to follow God no matter what the cost.

**Remember your calling and resolve to follow God no matter what the cost.**

## QUESTIONS FOR DISCUSSION AND PERSONAL APPLICATION

1. What is an area you want to influence? Evaluate whether the change you want to influence your leaders and organization to make is based on principle or preference. What is the principle behind the change? Is it important enough to cause the disruption and conflict it will bring? Is the end goal worth the battle? Are you committed even if it means great personal risk?

2. If you feel called to influence a situation but are facing doubt or danger, pray. Ask God for wisdom and courage. Ask for his perspective on your situation. Who might be a godly advisor who could pray with you?

3. If you are working under a difficult leader, how can you show respect and support for your leader and still initiate change? How specifically can you demonstrate love to your leader even when he or she may be resistant to your ideas?

_______________________________________________

_______________________________________________

_______________________________________________

_______________________________________________

_______________________________________________

_______________________________________________

_______________________________________________

CHAPTER SEVEN

# WHERE DO WE GO FROM HERE?

**God calls us to his service and places tremendous responsibilities on us . . . God wants to use us as he used his own Son.[57]**

**—— OSWALD CHAMBERS ——**

In Nigeria, whenever there is a road accident, onlookers at the scene discuss who is to blame. Very few take action to save those who are injured. We do the same in our churches, families, communities, and organizations. Of course, there are lots of problems in our organizations, churches, societies, and nations. But we have spent a lot of time complaining that the government is not doing anything. We have criticized the leaders for being corrupt or incapable. We have prayed to God for change. But we have felt helpless to do anything about it.

Let's stop for one moment. Pick up your phone. Take a selfie. What do you see?

You see the answer to these problems.

God created you. He calls the church his "body" of believers. We are his hands and feet. If we ask why God isn't doing anything about the situations we see, maybe he will ask us why we as his arms remain crossed at the chest and we as his feet refuse to go past the door!

When we see something wrong, something that doesn't work, or something that needs to be changed, God may be inviting us to be influencers. We need to open our eyes to these opportunities. We need to lead the change. How can we take responsibility and see how God has uniquely gifted us to do something about our situations?

Where can you have an influence starting right now? Let's look at some opportunities that could trigger you to have proactive influence in your relationships, churches, organizations, schools, workplaces, or communities:

- **Cause:** Perhaps you are motivated by injustice, human rights, poverty, public health, education, or economic empowerment. Is there a cause that you want to become involved in?
- **Compassion:** Maybe you know someone who is being mistreated, experiencing injustice, or simply going through a hard time. Who in your community is suffering physically or emotionally? Is there a situation that you are aware of or involved with that moves your heart with compassion?
- **Crisis:** Maybe you see a crisis. If you don't get involved and take action, someone may be harmed or integrity may be lost. You might need to take a risk. Do you see a crisis you need to be involved in?
- **Unexpected Opportunity:** Has God brought an unexpected opportunity into your path? Don't be reluctant; be ready to launch out into a new adventure with God. Maybe God has brought this opportunity to you for such a time as this. Be courageous and excited that God has considered you worthy to take up this task!
- **Question:** Perhaps you have questions: "Why do we do what we do? Why do we do it in the way that we do it? Are we doing the right thing or the best thing? Are we looking for the right things for the future?" Is there a question you would like to respectfully ask your leader?
- **Appeal:** If you have asked questions and suggested things that could be different but nothing is happening, you might want to respectfully appeal. You could propose a plan to them, give an alternative suggestion, or propose a trial with a definite time limit. Could you appeal to your leaders to test a different way for a time?

Just like the men and women in the Bible we have seen, you can influence those in power. You may be young. You may not have an official position. But leadership is not position. Leadership is influence.

**Leadership is not position. Leadership is influence.**

Don't worry if it seems like your influence is small, or things take time to change. Step by step, you can achieve small victories. You can move things in the right direction. The momentum can build for more change in the future. Stop sitting on the sidelines. Be strong and courageous! Step forward. Speak out. Seek lasting change.

God's method in every generation is using people like you and me. What if he is not looking for your parents or teachers or politicians to do something? What if he doesn't need you to be a prophet or apostle or CEO or founder to do something? You who may hold no position in your organization or community – you are a powerful weapon in God's hand to influence your generation for his glory. Are you willing to let God use you?

## QUESTIONS FOR DISCUSSION AND PERSONAL APPLICATION

1. What specific issue or concern can you identify as an area you want to influence?

2. What might be the first steps that you should take to begin to do something about this issue?

3. Who might be the key people, both peers and leaders alike, that you could begin to influence to become involved and help address this issue?

4. Write out a plan of action to incorporate the answers to the questions above. Include a time for starting these steps and a deadline for completing the initial part of the process.

_______________________________________________
_______________________________________________
_______________________________________________
_______________________________________________
_______________________________________________
_______________________________________________
_______________________________________________

5. Who can you share this plan with? This person should be one who can help keep you accountable and pray for you.

_______________________________________________
_______________________________________________
_______________________________________________
_______________________________________________
_______________________________________________
_______________________________________________
_______________________________________________

# ENDNOTES

1 Gary J. Bredfeldt, *Great Leader Great Teacher: Recovering the Biblical Vision for Leadership* (Chicago, IL: Moody Publishers, 2006), 61.

2 James O'Toole, *Leading Change: The Argument for Values-Based Leadership* (San Francisco, CA: Jossey-Bass, 1995), 11.

3 O'Toole, 11.

4 "Influence," accessed July 5, 2014, http://www.merriam-webster.com/dictionary/influence.

5 Heather Stagl, "Three Signs You've Crossed the Line From Influence to Manipulation," accessed July 5, 2014. http://www.enclaria.com/2011/03/08/three-signs-youve-crossed-the-line-from-influence-to-manipulation/.

6 J. Robert Clinton, *The Making of a Leader: Recognizing the Lessons and Stages of Leadership Development* (Singapore: NavPress, 1988), 14.

7 Serge Moscovici; Carol Sherrard and Greta Heinz, trans., *Social Influence and Social Change* (London: Academic Press, 1976), 68.

8 From James M. Kouzes and Barry Z. Posner, *The Leadership Challenge: How to Make Extraordinary Things Happen in Organizations* (San Francisco, CA: Jossey Bass, 2002), xii.

9 Maria Elena Duron, "Earn the Right to be Heard," accessed February 3, 2020, https://www.thepersonalbrandingblog.com/earn-the-right-to-be-heard/.

10 Adapted from Allan R. Cohen and David L. Bradford, *Influence Without Authority* (Hoboken, NJ: John Wiley & Sons, 2005), 91.

11 Of course, any of these can be used with wrong motives in order to ingratiate oneself to his or her leader or to gain something for oneself. However, we are assuming that the influencer is doing these things out of a desire to serve others and for their good.

12 John Jusu, ed. "Ubuntu." *Africa Study Bible* (Wheaton, IL: Oasis International Ltd, 2016), 1894.

13 Max De Pree, *Leadership Is an Art* (New York, NY: Doubleday, 2004), 25. De Pree's book is aimed at a leader who has an official organizational position. However, much of what he writes about leadership can also be applied to the influencer who leads without position.

14 John C. Maxwell and Jim Dornan, *Becoming a Person of Influence* (Nashville, TN: Thomas Nelson Publishers, 1997), 111.

15 Oswald Chambers, *My Utmost for His Highest*, (Uhrichsville, OH: Barbour & Company, Inc., 1935), 217.

16 Hyrum W. Smith, *The 10 Natural Laws of Successful Time and Life Management: Proven Strategies for Increased Productivity and Inner Peace* (New York, NY: Warner Books, Inc, 1994), 204.

17 Philip E. Morrison, *The Multi-Church Pastor* (Allentown, PA: Gratia Veritas Publishers, 2004), 39.

18 As cited by Michael Luo, "Preaching the Word and Quoting the Voice," *New York Times*, February 26, 2006 and quoted by MaryKate Morse, *Making Room for Leadership, Power, Space and Influence* (Downers Grove, IL: InterVarsity Press, 2008), 155.

19 A. B. Bruce, *The Training of the Twelve: How Jesus Christ Found and Taught the 12 Apostles; A Book of New Testament Biography* (Pantianos Classics, 2018), 14.

20 Spencer Johnson, *Who Moved My Cheese?* (London: Ebury Publishing, 1999), 91.

21 Robert Coleman, *The Master Plan of Evangelism* (Old Tappan, NJ: Fleming H. Revell Company, 1982), 36-37.

22 Michael J. Gorman, *Cruciformity: Paul's Narrative Spirituality of the Cross* (Grand Rapids, MI: William B. Eerdmans Publishing Company, 2001), 283.

23 Robert Coleman, *The Master Plan of Evangelism*, 36-37.

24 Gottfried Osei-Mensah, *Wanted: Servant Leaders* (Accra, Ghana: Africa Christian Press, 1990), 44, 53.

25 This section was inspired by reflections on Kouzes and Posner's book, *The Leadership Challenge*, in the following blogpost: John Deisher, "Leading Through Influence," April 1, 2010, http://hobnobconnect.wordpress.com/2010/04-01/leading-through-influence/.

26 "Defeated" is the English Standard Version translation. The New International Version translates 1 Samuel 13:3, "Jonathan attacked the Philistine outpost at Geba . . ."

27 As quoted by Maxwell and Dornan, *Becoming a Person of Influence*, 67.

28 Kouzes and Posner, *The Leadership Challenge*, 14.

29 MaryKate Morse, *Making Room for Leadership, Power, Space and Influence*, 113.

30 Adapted from Lewis Carroll, *Alice's Adventures in Wonderland* (New York, NY: Avenel Books, Crown Publishers, Inc., n.d.), 29.
Carroll's original lines are:
"Would you tell me, please, which way ought I to walk from here?"
"That depends a good deal on where you want to get to," said the Cat.
"I don't much care where – " said Alice.
"Then it doesn't matter which way you walk," said the Cat.

31 Faustin Ntamushobora, *From Trials to Triumphs: The Voice of Habakkuk to the Suffering African Christian* (Eugene, OR: Wipf and Stock Publishers, 2009), 61.

32 Cohen and Bradford, *Influence Without Authority*, 234.

33 Kibugua K. Kariithi and Dennis O. Tongoi, eds., *Building a Prosperous Kenya: A Perspective for the Church: God's Primary Agency for Social Transformation* (Nairobi, Kenya: Christians for a Just Society, 2005), 14.

34 Larry Bossidy and Ram Charan, *Execution: The Discipline of Getting Things Done* (New York, NY: Crown Business, 2002), 5.

35 Ibrahim Omondi, *Changing the Political Landscape of A Nation* (Nairobi, Kenya: MvuleAfrica Publishers, 2011), 144.

36 David Greenburg as quoted in Dave Zielinski, "Leading Without Authority," accessed September 25, 2014, Accessed June 9, 2020, http://www.toastmasters.org/~/media/19FFD274E9594264AC48E98D47E67226.ashx.

37 John C. Maxwell, *Good Leaders Ask Great Questions*, (New York, Centre Street Hachette Book Group: 2014), 4-14.

38 Maxwell and Dornan, *Becoming a Person of Influence*, 83-84.

39 I am indebted to Jan Olander for sharing these questions with me which were used by her college Public Speaking class lecturer.

40 Michael Zigarelli, *Influencing Like Jesus: 15 Biblical Principles of Persuasion* (Nashville, TN: B & H Publishing Group, 2008), 112.

41 Moscovici, *Social Influence and Social Change*, 27.

42 Ibid., 26.

43 As quoted by Michael Theriault, *Write to Influence: Quick Guides for Managers* (Toronto, Canada: WoodStone Press, 2012). Kindle edition, part 1.

44 Keshavan Nair, *A Higher Standard of Leadership: Lessons from the Life of Gandhi* (San Francisco, CA: Barrett-Koehler Publishers, 1997), xii.

45 Wangari Maathai, *The Challenge for Africa* (London: Arrow Books, 2009), 19.

46 Jim Herrington, Mike Bonem, and James H. Furr, *Leading Congregational Change: A Practical Guide for the Transformational Journey* (San Francisco, CA: Jossey-Bass Publishers, 2000), 90-91.

47 Moscovici, *Social Influence and Social Change*, 98.

48 Ibid., 110.

49 Barbara G. Wheeler, et al, "Leadership that Works," *Auburn Studies*, December 2010, 11.

50 Dallas Willard, *Renovation of the Heart* (Colorado Springs, CO: NavPress, 2002), 231-232.

51 De Pree, *Leadership Is an Art*, 70.

52 Hannah Hutyra, "Martin Luther King Jr. Quotes: In His Own Words," *Birmingham Times* (Birmingham, AL), January 15, 2018. https://www.birminghamtimes.com/2018/01/some-of-dr-martin-luther-king-jr-s-profound-quotes/.

53 The idea for this came from Ted Engstrom and Paul Cedar, *Compassionate Leadership: Rediscovering Jesus' Radical Leadership Style* (Ventura, CA: Regal Books, 2006), 127.

54 Jack Mezirow, "A Transformation Theory of Adult Learning," in *Annual Adult Education Research Conference (AERC) Proceedings* 31 (1990):141-146, accessed March 23, 2020, https://files.eric.ed.gov/fulltext/ED357160.pdf#page=153.

55 Ntamushobora, *From Trials to Triumphs*, 10, 11.

56 Ibid., 20.

57 Oswald Chambers, *My Utmost for His Highest*, 262.

# ABOUT THE AUTHORS

**Philip E. Morrison** pastored in the US for 14 years before moving to Kenya in 1992. As a lecturer at Moffat Bible College, he became passionate about equipping under-resourced pastors who are responsible for multiple congregations. As a result, he founded The Multi-Church Pastor Institute to mentor and train these pastors. He received a Doctor of Ministry degree from Africa International University and currently serves with Africa Inland Mission as the Child Safety Assistant. He is the author of six other books. He is married to Jan, has six children, and has five grandchildren.

**Hankuri Tawus Gaya** is a dynamic youth pastor and a campus missionary. He is passionate about challenging "just one soul" to become all that God has created it to be and make the world God's dream place. He holds a MDiv from Theological College of Northern Nigeria (TCNN) in addition to his training in accountancy. He is the author of 18 books including: *Discipling the Campus, You Can Transform your Campus, You Can Move Forward, Persecution to Promoting Christlikeness, The Purpose-Driven Corper,* and *The Kingdom-Driven Student.*

He presently serves as an Area Director and Strategic Plan Officer in Nigeria Fellowship of Evangelical Students (NIFES) a member movement of International Fellowship of Evangelical Students (IFES). He is also a faculty member of the NIFES Training Institute and a National Facilitator of Langham Preaching Nigeria, a ministry of John Stott committed to promoting expository Bible preaching around the world.

He is happily married to Faith Butmak. They are blessed with three daughters: Vinawar (God's gift), Shisa (God's Peace), and Khaala (God's Joy).

# More books by Philip E. Morrison

**FALLING ASLEEP IN THE LAP OF DELILAH: LESSONS ON FINISHING WELL FROM THE LIFE OF SAMSON**

It is never too late to start the process of finishing well. *Falling Asleep in the Lap of Delilah* is a treasure trove of wisdom on finishing the race of life well.

Facing the final stages of life, career, or ministry can be daunting and instil deep fear – a fear that can cause even the most devout Christian leader to make poor choices, compromise their faith, and damage their legacy. But as Dr Morrison shows, it's never too late to start finishing well.

Morrison's thoughtful insights and powerful meditations on the life of Samson, Israel's notorious strong-man judge, and just how he ended up falling asleep in Delilah's lap, can guide you in preserving your relationship with God and with others, enabling you to finish your race to hear, "Well done, good and faithful servant."

- QUESTIONS PASTORS ASK
- SEVEN SURPRISES FOR THE PASTOR
- THE MULTI-CHURCH PASTOR
- STEWARDSHIP OF TIME
- FOR OUR CHILDREN! FOR OUR CHURCH!
- STAYING ON COURSE: SELF-CARE FOR CHILD SAFETY WORKERS

**CONFLICT RESOLUTION IN THE CHURCH**

**(With Chris Mwalw'a)**

This book is an answer to the great need the church has for a practical approach to conflict resolution in the church. It focuses on scripturally-based, peace-making attitudes within the African church context.

OASIS INTERNATIONAL PUBLISHING

oasisinternationalpublishing.com | oasisinternational.co

READ A SNEAK PREVIEW OF

# Falling Asleep in the Lap of Delilah

# PROLOGUE

"How did this man come to this place?" she wondered looking intently at the face of the man whose head lay heavily in her lap. Her gaze was hard to read, as it was a mixture of amused amazement that this famous foe was so trusting and so vulnerable. She ran her finger through one of the ringlets of his long hair and noticed that it was flecked with grey. She studied his face and for the first time observed the slight wrinkling of skin. He was not a young man but he was a powerful man still in his prime.

Delilah did not love him, but he fascinated her. She did not hate him either and rather enjoyed the game of wits they had been playing. What *was* the key to the amazing strength of this Israelite man? The truth of this question had been her quest – and now she had it, and with it, a huge reward. She smiled in satisfaction. Soon, it would be all over, and she would win . . . when the barber came.

CHAPTER 1

# THE ISSUE OF SPIRITUAL COLDNESS OR "FALLING ASLEEP IN THE LAP OF DELILAH"[7]

I am sitting outside. It is warm. This is significant because our home of stone and concrete construction is quite cold. In fact, it is colder inside the house than outside. We are coming to the end of our winter here in Nairobi. People don't usually think of Africa being cold – but it can be. The winter months of June–August are often grey and overcast – and sometimes damp. The cold creeps into the very structure of our ground floor flat and settles there for the season. But I am sitting outside. The rays of the sun soften the edges of the cold blanket we have been living under and I revel in the warmth.

I wonder how many people are like this? They are cold on the inside while many around them are warm and vibrant. What causes the frigidness of the heart and soul? What causes the natural warmth of a child's sunny disposition to gradually succumb to the numbness of a frost-

---

7 This title is taken from the following lines from Bennett, 279: "Hast thou sought joys in some creature comfort? Look not below God for happiness; fall not asleep in Delilah's lap."

encrusted inner being? Where does the childish delight of life and wonder go? How do the bright embers of enthusiasm fade? What causes the awe of each new adventure to lose its appeal? And how does a child's openness to God and things spiritual close tightly shut?

Perhaps, it comes as one suffers disappointment, broken promises, unfulfilled dreams, injustice, and abuse. And so, the heart grows cold and an impervious shell of icy-protectiveness forms a frigid zone inside one's soul. Without the reception of love's warmth the inner man becomes an artic wasteland. And yet the person in the pain of spiritual coldness will seek comfort for his or her soul even if it means lowering standards and compromising values.

One day I visited a pastor during the middle of the week and after some conversation we went into the empty sanctuary and knelt at the front of the church to pray. As we prayed, he poured out his heart and urgently pleaded with the Lord, "God, I want your power upon my life." A number of years later he had left his wife, divorced, and married another woman.

How does one come to this place? That question could be asked of many men and women found in compromising positions. Many who have been servants of God with fruitful ministries and have been used by him for the salvation of souls and the building up of the body of Christ have later grown cold and walked away from their calling.

What was the path of failure and faithlessness that led them to turn away from what they had proclaimed to believe? The answer to that question has many parts and can lead in many directions. There are many possible causes contributing to compromise. Some may be common to all; some may be unique to one. But each cause can stand as a warning to others.

Such a warning comes from the life of Samson. He was a man set apart from birth by God for a unique service and the deliverance of his people. He was given great strength. He possessed a keen intellect and used his gifts to fulfil his divine calling that was declared to his parents at the announcement of his birth by the angel of the Lord who said, "he will begin the deliverance of Israel from the hands of the Philistines" (Judges 13:5).

And yet we find him falling asleep in the lap of Delilah, the Philistine woman who fascinated Samson and eventually led him to his downfall. This is a picturesque phrase used of a man who was chosen by God to be the leader of his people. It is also a phrase that should warn all of us about the wiles of the world that would woo God's people into temptation and sin.

In this study we will look at various dangers that eventually led Samson to Delilah's lap – and which could lead us there as well. This points to the truth that temptations are not new; they are just a variation on a theme as they take different forms from generation to generation and culture to culture. Satan is always intent on bringing to ruin God's servants and destroying their ministry. We would do well to carefully heed the lessons we can learn from the example of Samson's life, for in them we see those issues which will hinder us from finishing well.

# OASIS INTERNATIONAL

## *Satisfying Africa's Thirst for God's Word*

Our mission is to grow discipleship through publishing African voices.
**Go to oasisinternationalpublishing.com to learn more.**

**HIGHLY FAVOURED: OUR POWERFUL GOD'S COVENANT WITH YOU**
**Stuart J. Foster**
The God of the Bible is not unreliable or inaccessible like the spiritual beings in African traditional religions. He chooses to have a covenant relationship with his people and we do not have to earn God's favour.

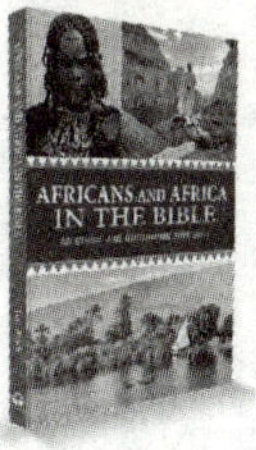


**AFRICANS AND AFRICA IN THE BIBLE**
**Tim Welch**
This book shows the presence and the participation of Africans in the biblical text, helping demonstrate that Christianity is not a "white man's religion" and that Christianity has deep roots in African soil.

**AFRICAN CHRISTIAN THEOLOGY REVISITED**
**Richard J. Gehman**
For all African Christians, *African Christian Theology Revisited* is a powerful plea to think through your faith in African contexts under the authority of the Word of God.

**PARENTING WITH PURPOSE & AFRICAN WISDOM**
**Gladys K. Mwiti**
This practical guide for Christians is a relevant, thoughtful presentation on the characteristics of parenting that delivers results.

**ANSWERS FOR YOUR MARRIAGE**
**Bruce and Carol Britten**
Offers practical insights to marriage issues and facts on sex, pregnancy, family planning, child-raising, money issues, adultery, HIV, and sex-related diseases. If your marriage is in despair, look to this book for some answers for your marriage.

**LEARNING TO LEAD**
**Richard J. Gehman**
With its discussion questions and practical applications, this book will guide you to obtaining character and skills, and help you become an effective Christian leader. It was written from the living experience of African leaders, and it has been shaped by 36 years of training church leaders in Kenya.

**HABITS OF HIGHLY EFFECTIVE CHRISTIANS**
**Ron Meyers**
In today's world of rushed deadlines and hurried lives, it's easy to forget that the Bible holds principles that provide a proper foundation for living. Learn about 17 habits that can help you lead a more fulfilling, healthy life both professionally and personally. Challenge how you think about the way we live in the 21st century.

**BIBLICAL CHRISTIANITY IN MODERN AFRICA**
**Wilbur O'Donovan**
*Biblical Christianity in Modern Africa* describes the major issues facing the church in Africa and offers suggestions on how these problems can be overcome.

OASIS INTERNATIONAL PUBLISHING

oasisinternationalpublishing.com | oasisinternational.com